MW00399169

DOVER · THRIFT · EDITIONS

Women's Writings on Christian Spirituality

EDITED BY
MOLLY HAND

DOVER PUBLICATIONS, INC.
Mineola, New York

DOVER THRIFT EDITIONS

GENERAL EDITOR: MARY CAROLYN WALDREP
EDITOR OF THIS VOLUME: ALISON DAURIO

Copyright

Copyright © 2013 by Dover Publications, Inc.
All rights reserved.

Bibliographical Note

Women's Writings on Christian Spirituality, first published in 2013,
contains a new selection of works made by Molly Hand, who also
provided the biographical information which precedes each chapter.

International Standard Book Number

ISBN-13: 978-0-486-48445-7
ISBN-10: 0-486-48445-9

Manufactured in the United States by Courier Corporation
48445901   2013
www.doverpublications.com

Introduction

Women writers are being read and studied now more than ever. Our understanding of the history of Christian spiritual texts is complicated and amplified by our increasing knowledge of women's roles in that history. While the writings included here are as diverse as the historical contexts in which they emerged, it is also possible to trace textual and spiritual relationships among these works and their authors. This volume provides an entry point to readers new to the history of women's spiritual writing as well as a site of further exploration for readers already familiar with some of these writers.

This is a historical anthology of women's religious writing. It begins with writings from the early church, including selections from Perpetua, Paula, and Dhuoda, and continues through the medieval (1100–1500) and early modern (1500–1800) periods, into our current era. Though these selections merit study within their contexts, one need not be a historian, literary scholar, or theologian in order to appreciate the strength of Kassia's writings, the subtlety of Julian of Norwich's theology, or the political daring of Anna Trapnel's prophecies. A brief preface to each of the selections below provides a biographical sketch as well as a sense of context for the passage.

What do these women have in common? What do these selections have in common? In some ways, the answer to both questions is very little. The sweep of history, from Perpetua's experience as a martyr in the early church to Anne Lamott's journey raising her son in the California Bay

area, is vast, as is the geographical scope—from Constantinople
and Bethlehem to France, Sweden, and the United States.
What could Kassia possibly have in common with Nancy
Mairs, or with Aemilia Lanyer?

In our postmodern era, we understand that women are not
the "weaker sex," do not share inherent perspectives, innate
"feminine" characteristics, or some built-in "womanly" notions
by sheer virtue of being women. People's perspectives, their
experiences as gendered beings, and their abilities to read,
write, or speak in any given context are all culturally determined. Encountering the itinerant prophesying visionary
woman Margery Kempe would have been much stranger for
her contemporaries in the late fourteenth century than it
would have been for London's citizens to hear Margaret Fell
Fox preaching two centuries later. Cultural context deter-
mines reception, as well as the ability to be read or heard in
the first place. Phillis Wheatley's ability to publish her work
and have it received by a broad audience required that she
have white patrons offering their approbation in writing; her
experience of public writing was mediated because of race.
Other women, like Anna Trapnel, Angela of Foligno, and
numerous others, told their spiritual narratives and visionary
experiences to a male confessor or amanuensis. Yet, however
mediated these texts may be, one way or another, these
women writers overcame barriers of gender, class, race, geography, and more—and conveyed, in writing, their remarkable
voices and experiences.

Perhaps this overcoming of obstacles is what creates the
connections that, despite the irretrievable differences
among these women and their contexts, exist among their
texts. What Kassia, Nancy Mairs, and Aemilia Lanyer have
in common is their defense of women, their questioning of
the patriarchal structure of the church and the broader culture, their critique of misogynistic views that were, if not
espoused, then underwritten, by church doctrine and dominant culture more broadly. As many women in this volume

expressed outrage at male-dominated society's injustices towards women, so, we must also remember, were many of these women aided and supported by male members of their religious communities. Though several authors included here were enclosed or secluded in the cloister, many of these women did not enter convents, joining lay religious communities instead. Though they may each have had different reasons for joining lay orders, they were afforded greater agency and the ability to be active in their communities in ways that nuns could not be. Beguines, like Mechthild of Madgeburg and Hadewijch of Brabant, formed their own lay spiritual communities in Europe; Catherine of Siena and Angela of Foligno were in Dominican and Franciscan Third (lay) Orders, respectively. Some of these women were powerful indeed. Catherine and Birgitta of Sweden became advisors to popes and powerful clergy. Anna Trapnel almost certainly inspired a degree of discomfort, if not fear, in the heart of Oliver Cromwell.

Just as fascinating as these diverse situations by which women entered religious communities and the public sphere of letters, are the direct connections among some of these writers. To mention only a few, Margery Kempe admired Birgitta of Sweden and visited Julian of Norwich. Flannery O'Connor praised Simone Weil. Quaker women Katharine Evans and Margaret Fell Fox were contemporaries. Gertrude the Great resided at the same convent at Helfta where Mechthild of Madgeburg spent her later years finishing Book 7 of *The Flowing Light of the Godhead*. Elisabeth of Schönau sought the approval of and exchanged letters with Hildegard of Bingen. Textually, spiritually, and historically intertwined, the writers and texts in this volume offer us a glimpse of a vast transhistorical community that defies contexts, orthodoxies, and expectations.

The selections that comprise this collection exemplify each writer's style and voice. I have included selections less frequently anthologized in order to provide readers a fresh look at some writers whose work is often anthologized, and I have included selections from writers that have not yet been included in historical anthologies of women's spiritual writings. I hope these selections will serve as a starting point for many readers, because there is so much more to read than the small space of this book can contain.

I was introduced to a number of these texts by Nancy Bradley Warren when I was working on my doctoral degree in English literature; my interest in women's spiritual writing of the medieval and early modern eras was sparked by our readings and discussions in her class. I hope this volume will bring these women writers to the attention of new readers who will find inspiration in their distinctive voices, styles, theologies, strength of spirit, and political outspokenness.

MOLLY HAND, *Editor*

Table of Contents

Perpetua   1
Paula   7
Dhuoda of Septimania   12
Kassia   18
Hildegard of Bingen   22
Elisabeth of Schönau   26
Beatrijs of Nazareth   38
Mechthild of Magdeburg   43
Hadewijch of Brabant   49
Angela of Foligno   53
Gertrude the Great   61
Birgitta of Sweden   67
Catherine of Siena   72
Julian of Norwich   76
Christine de Pisan   84
Margery Kempe   88
Teresa of Avila   95
Grace Mildmay   108
Mary Sidney Herbert   113
Aemilia Lanyer   118
Eleanor Davies   124
Anne Bradstreet   133
Margaret Fell Fox   137
Katharine Evans   146
Mary Cary   151
Anna Trapnel   159
Phillis Wheatley   166

Jarena Lee   171
Maria W. Stewart   178
Emily Dickinson   187
Therèse of Lisieux   190
Simone Weil   195
Flannery O'Connor   202
Nancy Mairs   207
Anne Lamott   214
Heidi Neumark   220

Acknowledgments   225

Perpetua
(d. 203)

Perpetua was a third-century martyr, whose travails are recorded in *The Passion of St. Perpetua*. Perpetua dictated her account, which was then commented upon and edited by Tertullian. Like several other women whose work is included in this volume, Perpetua channeled the spirit of God, experienced visions, and suffered persecution (and ultimately execution) for her beliefs. Her experiences are mediated through a male author/editor, but as with many of her later counterparts, it is possible to hear a compelling individual voice bodied forth from this account.

III. "From the time that I joined my companions my father not only wished to turn me from my purpose with arguments, but also persisted in trying to break down my faith through his affection for me. 'Father,' said I, 'do you see this vessel lying here—a jug, or whatever it is?' 'I see it,' said he. 'Can one call anything by any other name than what it is?' 'No,' said he. 'So neither can I call myself anything else but what I am, a Christian.' Angered at this word my father threw himself upon me as though to tear out my eyes; but he only shook me, and forthwith was overcome along with the devil's arguments. Then for a few days, because I missed my father, I gave thanks to God and was refreshed by his absence. In that brief space of time we were baptized; and the Spirit intimated to me that I was not to expect anything else from my baptism but sufferings of the flesh. A few days later we were received into the prison, and I

1

shuddered because I had never experienced such gloom. O awful day! fearful heat arising from the crowd and from the jostling of the soldiers! Finally I was racked with anxiety for my infant there. Then Tertius and Pomponius, blessed deacons who were ministering to us, arranged by bribery for us to go forth for a few hours and gain refreshment in a better part of the prison. And so going forth we all were free to attend to ourselves. I suckled my child, who was already weak from want of nourishment. In my anxiety for him I spoke to my mother, and comforted my brother, and entrusted my child to them. And I pined excessively because I saw them pining away because of me. For many days I suffered these anxieties; and I then gained the point that my child should remain with me in the prison. And immediately I gained strength, being relieved from anxiety about the child; and my prison suddenly became to me a palace, so that I preferred to be there rather than anywhere else."

IV. "Then my brother said to me, 'My lady sister, thou art already in such a position of dignity that thou mayest ask both for a vision and that it may be shown thee whether we are to suffer or to be released.' And I, who knew myself to be holding converse with the Lord, for Whose sake I had experienced such great trials, faithfully promised him, saying, 'To-morrow, I will tell thee.' And I prayed, and this vision was shown to me: I see a brazen ladder of wondrous size reaching up to heaven; narrow, moreover, so that only one could go up it at once, and on its sides every kind of iron instrument fixed—swords, lances, hooks, daggers—so that if one went up carelessly, or not fixing one's attention upwards one would be torn, and pieces of one's flesh would be left on the iron implements. There was also lying under the ladder a dragon of wondrous size, which laid snares for those climbing it, and frightened them from the ascent. Now Saturus went up first. He had given himself up voluntarily after our arrest on our account, because he had taught us the faith, and he had not been present on the occasion of our trial. When he got to the top of the ladder he turned and said to me, 'Perpetua, I am waiting for you; but take care that that dragon does not bite you.' And I said, 'In the name of Jesus Christ he shall not hurt me.' And the dragon, as if afraid of me, slowly thrust his head underneath the ladder itself; and I trod upon his head as if I were treading on the first step. And I went up and saw a large space of garden, and in the midst a man with white hair sitting, in the garb of a shepherd, tall, milking sheep; and a white-robed host standing round him. And he lifted his head and saw me, and said, 'Welcome, child'; and he called me and gave me a piece of the cheese which he was making, as it were a small mouthful, which I received with joined hands and ate; and all those around said 'Amen.' And at the sound of the word I awoke, still tasting something sweet.

"This vision I told at once to my brother, and we understood that we were about to suffer martyrdom, and we began to give up every earthly hope."

V. "After a few days a rumor ran round that our case was to be heard. Moreover my father came up from the city, worn out with disgust; and he came to break down my faith, saying, 'Daughter, pity my grey hairs; pity your father, if I am worthy to be called father by you, if I have brought you up with my own hands to your present comely age, if I have preferred you to all your brothers: do not make me disgraced before men. Behold your brothers; behold your mother and your aunt; look at your son, who cannot live without you. Alter your determination: do not cut us off entirely; for no one of us will ever hold up his head again if anything happens to you.' This my father said out of his affection for me, kissing my hands, and throwing himself at my feet, and with tears calling me not 'daughter' but 'lady.' And I was distressed at my father's state, for he alone of my kindred would not rejoice at my martyrdom. So I comforted him, saying, 'This will be done on that stage which God has willed: for know that we have not been placed in our own power but in God's.' And he left me very sorrowfully."

VI. "On another day, when we were breakfasting, we were suddenly carried off to our trial, and we were taken to the forum. The rumor of it immediately got about the neighborhood and an immense crowd gathered. We go up into the dock. The others when questioned confessed. Then my turn came. And my father appeared on the spot with my boy, and drew me down from the step, praying to me, 'Pity thy child.' Then Hilarian the procurator, who at that time was administering the government in place of the proconsul Minucius Timinianus, deceased, said, 'Spare thy father's grey hairs; spare thy infant boy. Sacrifice for the safety of the Emperor.' And I replied, 'I do not sacrifice.' 'Art thou a Christian?' asked Hilarian; and I said, 'I am.' And when my father persisted in endeavoring to make me recant, he was ordered down by Hilarian and beaten with a rod. And I felt it as keenly as though I had been struck myself; and I was sorry for his miserable old age.

"Then he pronounced sentence against us all, and condemned us to the beasts; and we joyfully went down to the prison. Then, because my child had been accustomed to be suckled by me and to remain with me in the prison, I sent Pomponius the deacon immediately to my father for the child, but he refused to give it up. And somehow God willed it that neither the child any longer desired the breasts, nor did they cause me pain; and thus I was spared anxiety about the child and personal discomfort."

VII. VIII. [In these sections Perpetua narrates the substance of two further visions vouchsafed to her, one whilst all were engaged in prayer, and the other on a day when the imprisoned confessors were placed in the stocks.]

IX. "Then, after a few days, Pudens the adjutant, the governor of the prison, began to make much of us, perceiving our fortitude, and let a number of people in to see us, so that we and they were eventually comforted. Now as the day of our exhibition drew near, my father came again to me, worn out with disgust, and began to tear out his beard and throw it on the ground, and to prostrate himself, and to plead with me on account of his years, and to utter such taunts as to turn the world upside down. I grieved for his unhappy old age."

X. "On the day before we were to fight, I saw in a vision Pomponius the deacon coming hither to the door of the prison and knocking violently. And I went out and opened to him. He was clothed in a loose white robe, and wore embroidered shoes. And he said to me, 'Perpetua, we are waiting for you; come.' And he took my hand, and we began to traverse rough and winding passages. At last with difficulty we arrive panting at the amphitheatre, and he led me into the middle of the arena, and said to me, 'Fear not: I will be here with thee, and will assist thee.' And he departed. And I behold a vast crowd eagerly watching. And because I knew that I was to be given to the beasts, I wondered why the beasts were not sent to me. And a certain Egyptian of terrible aspect came forth against me along with his assistants, ready to fight with me. There came also to me comely young men as my assistants and helpers. And I was smoothed down and changed my sex. And they began to rub me down with oil, as is customary for a contest. And I see that Egyptian opposite rolling in the dust. And a certain man came forth, of wondrous size, whose height was greater than the amphitheatre, wearing a loose purple robe with two broad stripes over the middle of his breast, and embroidered shoes wrought of gold and silver. He carried a rod like a fencing-master, and a green branch on which were golden apples. Calling for silence he said, 'This Egyptian, if he conquer her, shall kill her with the sword, but if she conquer him she shall receive this branch.' And he went away. And we approach each other, and begin to exchange blows. He was trying to catch me by the feet, but I was striking his face with my heels. And I was borne aloft in the air, and began to strike him as though I were not treading upon the ground. But when

I saw we were wasting time I joined my hands and interlocked my fingers. Then I caught him by the head, and he fell on his face and I trampled on his head. And the people began to shout, and my assistants to sing psalms. And I went up to the fencing-master and received the branch. And he gave me a kiss, and said to me, 'Daughter, peace be with thee.' And I began to walk with glory to the gate Sanavivaria. And I awoke; and I understood that I was destined not to fight with the beasts, but against the devil; but I knew that victory would be mine.

"I have brought this narrative up to the day before the show. If any one wishes, he may write what was done on the day itself."

Paula
(347–404)

Saint Paula was a daughter of a noble Roman family of the fourth century. She was acquainted with Saint Jerome, whose famous Latin translation of the bible, the Vulgate, would remain the seminal translation for centuries to come. After she became a widow, she and one of her daughters, Eustochium, traveled to the Holy Land. Paula founded a convent and monastery in Bethlehem. She died in Bethlehem in 404. This letter, from 386, depicts Bethlehem as a Christian utopia. Some explanatory footnotes from the source text are included.

II. To these places we have come, not as persons of importance, but as strangers, that we might see in them the foremost men of all nations. Indeed, the company of monks and nuns is a flower and a jewel of great price among the ornaments of the Church. Whoever may be the first men in Gaul hasten hither. The Briton, separated from our world,[1] if he has made any progress in religion, leaves the setting sun, and seeks a place known to him only by fame and the narrative of the Scriptures. Why need we mention the Armenians, the Persians, the nations of India and Ethiopia, and the neighboring country of Egypt, abounding in monks, Pontus and Cappadocia,[2]

---

[1] Virgil, Ecl. i. 67.
[2] Pontus and Cappadocia, two Roman provinces in Eastern Asia Minor; the former on the *Black Sea* coast, the latter between Pontus and Cilicia on the *Mediterranean* coast.

Cœle-Syria,[3] and Mesopotamia, and all the multitudes of the East, who, fulfilling the words of our Savior, "Wherever the carcass is, thither will the eagles be gathered together," flock into these places and display to us examples of diverse excellence?

III. Their speech differs, but their religion is one. There are almost as many choirs of psalm-singers as there are different nations. Among all this will be found what is, perhaps, the greatest virtue among Christians—no arrogance, no overweening pride in their chastity; all of them vie with one another in humility. Whoever is last is reckoned as first. In their dress there is no distinction, no ostentation. The order in which they walk in procession neither implies disgrace nor confers honor. Fasts also fill no one with pride, abstinence is not commended, nor is modest repletion condemned. Every man stands or falls by the judgment of his own Lord; no one judges another, lest he should be judged by the Lord. And here the practice of backbiting, so common in most countries, finds absolutely no place. Far from hence is luxury and self-indulgence.

IV. There are so many places of prayer in the city itself, that one day cannot suffice for visiting them all. However, to come to the village of Christ[4] and the inn of Mary (for everyone praises most that which he possesses), by what words, with what voice, can we describe to you the grotto of the Savior? That manger, too, wherein the babe wailed, is better honored by silence than by imperfect speech. Where are spacious porticos? Where are gilded ceilings? Where are houses decorated by the sufferings and labors of condemned

---

[3] The valley between *Lebanon* and *Anti-Lebanon*. It is mentioned by Jerome in the "Pil. of St. Paula," p. 3.
[4] Bethlehem.

wretches? Where are halls[5] built by the wealth of private men on the scale of palaces, that the vile carcass of man may move among more costly surroundings, and view his own roof rather than the heavens, as if anything could be more beauteous than creation?[6] Behold, in this little nook of the earth the Founder of the heavens was born; here He was wrapped in swaddling clothes, beheld by the shepherds, shown by the star, adored by the wise men.

VI. But in the village of Christ, as we said before, all is rusticity, and except for psalms, silence. Whithersoever you turn yourself, the ploughman, holding the plough-handle, sings Alleluia; the perspiring reaper diverts himself with psalms, and the vine-dresser sings some of the songs of David while he trims the vine with his curved knife. These are the ballads of this country, these are the love-songs, as they are commonly called; these are whistled by the shepherds, and are the implements of the husbandman. Indeed, we do not think of what we are doing or of how we look, but see only that for which we are longing.

VII. Oh, when will that time come when a breathless messenger shall bring us the news that our Marcella has reached the shore of Palestine, and all the choirs of monks, all the troops of nuns shall shout applause? We already are eager to start, and though no vehicle is expected, yet we wish to run to meet it. We shall clasp your hands, we shall behold your face, and shall scarcely be able to leave your long-wished-for embrace. When will that day come, when we shall be able to enter the grotto of our Savior?[6] to weep with our sister, and

---

[5] *"Basilicæ."* A basilica was a pagan secular building used for various purposes. Its special characteristics were the division into nave and aisles, and the clerestory lighting. The allusion here is to the large private halls in the mansions of the wealthy, which are described by Vitruvius, "De Arch.," vi. 3, 9.
[6] The "Grotto of the Nativity," at Bethlehem.

with our mother, in the Sepulcher of the Lord? Afterwards, to kiss the wood of the Cross, and on the Mount of Olives, together with our ascending Lord, to lift up our hearts and fulfill our vows? to see Lazarus come forth bound with grave clothes,[7] and to see the waters of Jordan, made more pure by the baptism of the Lord? And thence to go to the folds of the shepherds,[8] and pray in the tomb of David?[9] To behold Amos the prophet[10] even now lamenting on his rock with his shepherd's bugle-horn? To hasten to the tabernacles or tombs of Abraham, Isaac and Jacob, and their three noble wives?[11] To behold the fountain wherein the eunuch was baptized by Philip?[12] To go to Samaria, and adore with equal fervor the ashes of John the Baptist, of Elisha, and of Abdia? To enter the caves, wherein, in time of persecution and famine, troops of prophets were fed.

VIII. We shall go to Nazareth, and, according to the interpretation of its name, shall behold the flower[13] of Galilee. Not far from thence will be seen Cana, wherein the waters were turned into wine. We shall go on to Itabyrium,[14] and shall see the tabernacles of the Savior, not, as Peter would have built them, with Moses and Elias, but with the Father and the Holy

---

[7] The tomb of Lazarus was shown to the Bordeaux Pilgrim at Bethany; and the tomb and house of Mary and Martha to St. Paula.

[8] The "Tower Ader" of the Pilgrimage now *Beit Sahûr*, near Bethlehem.

[9] According to the Bordeaux Pilgrim, the Tomb of David was not far from the basilica at Bethlehem; according to "Antoninus Martyr," it was half a mile from the town.

[10] An allusion to Tekoa, *Kh. Tekûa*, the birthplace of Amos, and to the prophet's shepherd origin.

[11] At Hebron.

[12] The fountain is placed by the Bordeaux Pilgrim at Bethasora, Bethzur, now *Beit Sûr*, between Bethlehem and Hebron.

[13] The proper Hebrew name of Nazareth was *Nétzer*, a *shoot* or *sprout*. The comparison of Nazareth with a flower is not uncommon in the works of later pilgrims. Quaresmius compares it to a rose.

[14] Mount Tabor. The name occurs in the same form in the LXX. and Josephus.

Spirit. Thence we shall come to the Sea of Gennesareth, and shall see the five and four thousand men in the desert fed with five and seven loaves. Before us will appear the city of Naim,[15] at whose gates the widow's son was raised from the dead. We shall see, too, Hermoniim,[16] and the brook of Endor,[17] whereat Sisera was overcome. We shall also see Capharnaum, that familiar witness of the miracles of our Lord, and likewise the whole of Galilee. And then, accompanied by Christ, when we have returned to our grotto, after passing Silo[18] and Bethel,[19] and the other places in which the banners of the Church have been raised, as though to celebrate the victories of the Lord, we will sing constantly, we will often weep, we will pray without ceasing, and, wounded by the dart of our Savior, we will repeat together, "I have found Him whom my soul sought for; I will hold Him fast and will not let Him go."[20]

---

[15] Now *Nein*.
[16] Psalm xlii. 6. Probably *Jebel Dûhy.*
[17] An error for Kishon. Psalm lxxiii. 9, 10.
[18] Shiloh, *Seilûn.*
[19] *Beitîn.*
[20] Song of Solomon, iii. 4.

Dhuoda of Septimania
(c. 803–c. 843)

Dhuoda was married to Bernard, the Duke of Septimania, in 824. Close to the Carolingian court, Bernard and his family faced political trouble when the question of succession emerged. While Bernard engaged in political affairs, Dhuoda maintained their estate in the south of France. When their son, William, went to serve at the court of Charles the Bald, Dhuoda wrote the *Liber Manualis* for him. The excerpt below instructs William to display Christian conduct and attitudes. The source text's parenthetical references to biblical passages are included.

Pr.8.1. It is I, Dhuoda, who give you direction, my son William. I wish that, as you grow patiently in worthy virtues among those who fight alongside you, you may always be slow to speak, and slow to anger (James 1:19). If you grow angry, do so without sin. May it never happen that our merciful God grows angry in turn with you or—and may this also never befall—that you stray in your anger from the true path.

Therefore I direct you that, with gentleness, justice, and holiness, you perform your worldly service to him who, admonishing his faithful ones to shine with patience, says, In your patience you shall possess your souls (Luke 21:19). If you are patient, and if you restrain your thoughts and your tongue, you will be blessed. Your mind will be at peace, fearless everywhere, as if you were at a feast in the midst of many merrymaking companions. For it is written, a secure mind is like a continual feast (Prov. 15:15).

Pr.8.2. When you are well instructed by these and other examples, may you strive to act so peacefully that you may be found worthy to share the lot of blessedness with those of whom it is written, Blessed are the peacemakers: for they shall be called the children of God (Matt. 5:9). Surely a man should devote much effort to such a matter, so that—though he is the son of mortality—he may be found worthy to be called as well the son of the living God and to be established as the heir of that Lord's kingdom. If you are gentle and if you plow the furrow of good works, going forth always in honor, you will be found worthy to be joined with those of whom the Lord, granting a great inheritance for their praiseworthy manner, says, Blessed are the meek: for they shall possess the land (Matt. 5:4).

Pr.8.3. If you encounter a poor man, offer him as much help as you can, not only in words but also in deeds. I direct you likewise to offer generous hospitality to pilgrims, widows and orphans, children and indigents and to be quick to lift your hand to help those who you see are in need. As Scripture says, we are sojourners, immigrants and strangers, as were all our fathers (1 Par. 29:5; cf. Ps. 38:13) who passed upon the earth. Read Moses' admonition to the sons of Israel that they show brotherly compassion; he exhorted them strongly, saying: remember that you also were strangers and pilgrims in the land of Egypt (Deut. 10:19). Another man said of pilgrims and wayfarers, so that he might be their companion in his fraternal compassion and so that he might find others to be his successors in this great effort, my door was open to the traveler (Job 31:32). He said about orphans: I was the father of orphans and the judge of widows (Ps. 67:6; cf. Job 29:16). And again, and the cause which I knew not, I searched out most diligently (Job 29:16). You must not fail to have pity for the poor, my son, for God often hears their voices, as the

Psalmist says. He says, The Lord hath heard the desire of the poor (Ps. 9:17). And again, This poor man cried, and the Lord heard him (Ps. 33:7). For the poor man and the man in need cry out the Lord's name and praise him. We know that poverty and want are found not only among the least of men but also frequently, for many reasons, among the great. So it is that a rich man too may be in need. Why? Because his soul is wretchedly needy. And then there is the poor man who gathers riches with great ease. Or the rich man who envies the poor man, or the poor man who wishes to become rich, just as an unlettered man wishing to become learned may desire this completely but never accomplish it. Of such men a certain author says: "The rich and the poor man perish together, and are at once tortured by their need, the rich man because he does not give away what he has, and the poor man because he does not have it. When they sleep, they are oppressed by similar burdens: the former do not have the spirit of humility, nor do they find the blessed rest of the spirit of poverty" (cf. Gregory, Moralia in Job 15:56, 65, PL 75, 1114). They are restless and troubled for what is hateful to many. Someone says, my soul hateth . . . a poor man that is proud: a rich man that is a liar (Eccles. 25:3–4).

Pr.8.4. Opinions vary about differences between the rich and other rich men, and between the poor and other poor men. It was a rich, distinguished man who said, But I am a beggar and poor (Ps. 39:18). And again, humbling himself the more, he said, But I am a worm, and no man: the reproach . . . and the outcast of the people (Ps. 21:7).

Then again, woe is me, alas, my sojourning is prolonged (Ps. 119:5) too much. Setting aside his riches with the consolation of the Holy Ghost (Acts 9:31), returning to himself, he said, The Lord is my firmament, my refuge, and my deliverer (Ps. 17:3), and he is always prompt in being careful for me (Ps. 39:18). Therefore I joyfully confess his praise in the words of this poem: I will sing to the Lord, who giveth me good things

(Ps. 12:6). I will sing to the name of the Lord the most high (Ps. 7:18), that his law may be always fruitful in my mouth (cf. Ps. 33:2).

Pr.8.5. If so great a man spoke of himself as least among the small, lowliest of all, what of us? He hoped in the Lord, and that bountiful liberator freed him from all dangers. Surely those who have come before us, our forefathers and predecessors who called out to the Lord on account of their many worthy merits and placing their hope in him, were not confounded (Ps. 21:6) or led into disgrace but—as we believe—were filled with spiritual and material riches and in the end were saved. As the same author affirms, the houses of Abraham, Isaac, Israel, Moses, Aaron, and Levi, and others whose names I am not worthy to list or whose shoes to unfasten (cf. Luke 3:16)—men who had hope in the Lord and called out to him with all their heart, whom he brought . . . out of their distresses and led safely to the haven which they wished for (Ps. 106:28–30)—praised his greatness on earth and are blessed in the world to come. Confessing him, they say, Praise ye the God of gods . . . the Lord of lords (Ps. 135:2–3), praise him all kings of the earth and all people (Ps. 135:2–3), of all nations and languages (cf. Apoc. 5:9), for he is great and good: for his mercy endureth for time and eternity (Ps. 135:1). Since they and those who have come after them, believing as they did, confess and praise him, I urge you that you too love all the good things mentioned above and that, as an attentive reader and doer of good works, you strive to fulfill these last counsels, too, in the most worthy fashion.

Pr.8.6. Fear the Lord, and you will meet with such praise as the Psalmist offers. For he says, Blessed is the man that feareth the Lord (Ps. 111:1). As for whoever is found worthy to be filled with this fear, His seed shall be mighty upon earth . . . Glory and wealth shall be in his house through all things, and his justice will gleam forth for ever and ever (Ps. 111:2–3). If I were able, I would will it that what was true for them be true for you as well. As it is, I wish and pray that it may come to pass for you, my boy.

Pr.8.7. Love purity, and you will be the companion of him who is bright and gleaming, more splendid than any other. A certain author says, "Love chastity, boy, and you will be pure of sin". And another says: love chastity, young man: shining in it, you will give forth a rich fragrance. Pure of sin, you will cross the high clouds of heaven in your course. Follow this path, and you will share with the pure of heart that blessedness of the spirit about which you may read above. In Sion you may see (cf. Ps. 83:8) him who said, Blessed are the clean of heart, for they shall see God (Matt. 5:8).

Pr.8.8. Love the poor, and gather them to you. Do your duty to them at all times in the spirit of mildness and gentleness, lest you forget fraternal compassion for those who are beneath you. Always let your nobility be clothed in a suppliant heart, in the poverty of the spirit. Then you will be able to listen untroubled and to share in the kingdom with those of whom it is written, Blessed are the poor in spirit: for theirs is the kingdom of heaven (Matt. 5:3).

Pr.8.9. Love justice, so that you may be recognized as just in legal matters. For the Lord is just, and hath loved justice. He loves it always. His countenance beholds righteousness (Ps. 10:8). Another man loved it greatly long ago, and he directed that it be loved when he said, Love justice, you that are the judges of the earth (Wisd. 1:1). Yet another said, if in very deed you speak justice, judge right things (Ps. 57:2). It is written, for with what judgment you judge, you shall be judged (Matt. 7:2).

Therefore, my son William, avoid iniquity, love fairness, follow justice, and fear to hear the saying of the Psalmist: he that loveth iniquity hateth his own soul (Ps. 10:6). That Lord who is true and pure has given you a soul that is true, pure, and immortal, though in a fragile body. May it not befall you, then, to prepare evil snares for that soul, for the sake of desire for transient things, by doing or saying or consenting to acts of injustice or pitilessness. For many are tormented for the wrongdoings of others.

Be mindful, if you arrive at this point, of Elias and the rest. For a certain author says, "I sin with all sinners, if I do not correct them when I see them sinning." And another says, Lift not up the horn to the sinner (cf. Ps. 74:5). Whatever is passed over in lesser persons is demanded of those who are greater.

Kassia
(c. 810–c. 865)

Kassia was a Byzantine noblewoman who chose a monastic life, founding a convent in 843 and becoming its abbess. She was highly educated and produced a diverse body of creative and religious written work. Her hymns, some of which are included in Eastern Orthodox masses, are probably most well known, but she wrote poetry and prose as well. Though she faced persecution for her orthodox beliefs, including regard for Christian icons, by the iconoclast Emperor Theophilus, she remained vocal in her beliefs throughout her life.

These selections praise women who were significant in the evolution of the early church; compare, for example, to the selections from Christine de Pisan and Aemilia Lanyer in this volume. These hymns indicate the day and service at which they are meant to be sung.

Great-martyr Thekla (Sept. 24) at the Orthos

You rejected the earthly suitor and
    bride-chamber,
first among marytrs, Thekla,
and took a heavenly bridegroom, Christ
    our God.   5
You were not persuaded by a mother's
    coaxing,
but wisely followed Paul,

and lifted the banner of the Cross on
  your shoulders;   10
Thus the fire did not take hold of
  you,
you converted the savagery of the
  beasts to gentleness,
you destroyed the seals by your   15
  immersion in Christ
as in the Holy Baptism.
Since you were so outstanding in the
  noble struggle,
don't neglect to intercede unceasingly 20
  with the Lord
on behalf of those who faithfully
  commemorate
your ever-venerable memory.

The Pious Pelagia (Oct. 8) at Vespers

Wherever sin has become excessive,
grace has abounded even more,
as the Apostle teaches;
for with tears and prayers, Pelagia,
you have dried up the vast sea of   5
  sins,
and through penitence brought about
  the results acceptable to the
  Lord;
and now you intercede with him on 10
  behalf of our souls.

Line 3. The apostle is St. Paul; cf. Romans 5:20. (Translator's note)

The Great-martyr Barbara (Dec. 4) at the Orthos

The evil one has been dishonored,
defeated by a woman,
because he held the First-Mother

as an instrument of sin;
for the Logos of the Father,   5
simple and immutable,
as only he is known,
was made flesh of a Virgin
and removed from the curse of Eve and Adam,
Christ deservedly crowned Barbara the   10
    Martyr,
and through her gives to the world a
    means of atonement and great
    mercy.

Lines 1-9. The Virgin Mary, by giving birth to Christ, defeated the evil serpent, who tempted Eve. (Translator's note)

Martyr Agathe (Feb. 5) at Vespers

An incredible wonder occurred
at the martyrdom of the all-glorious
    Agathe
and martyr of Christ, God, one equal
    to Moses';   5
for he framed the laws of his people
    on the mountain,
when he received the God-written
    Commandments
inscribed on a tablet;   10
in this instance, an angel from heaven
placed a tablet on her tomb
on which was inscribed:
"Holy mind, possessed of free choice,
honor from God, and deliverance of the   15
    country."

Eudokia of the Samarians (March 1) at Vespers

The pious and martyred one
left behind the pleasure and

> complexities of life,
> and lifting the cross on her
> > shoulders,   5
> came to be wed to you, Christ,
> and with wails of tears cried out,
> "Don't cast me, the harlot, aside,
> you who purges the dissolute;
> don't overlook my tears for my debts,   10
> but receive me as you did that harlot
> who brought myrrh to you,
> so I too might hear:
> 'Your faith has saved you,
> go in peace.'"   15

Line 9. The reference is to Mary Magdalene, the sinful penitent woman
who washed Christ's feet with her tears and wiped them dry with her hair.
Luke 7:36–50.

Lines 12-13. Luke 7:50. (Translator's notes)

Hildegard of Bingen
(1098–1179)

Saint Hildegard was a visionary woman, a prolific
writer, and the founding abbess of the Benedictine
community at Bingen. She preached publicly,
exhorting monks and clergy to seek reform within
their communities and institutions. Like Margery
Kempe and Anna Trapnel, she took her message on
the road, preaching at various locations to monastic
as well as public audiences. The trilogy known as the
Scivias is her best known and most studied work.
The three books describe and expound upon her
prophetic visions. Hildegard wrote several other
voluminous texts, including two scientific and medical treatises, a collection of religious songs, additional religious and visionary works, and myriad
letters. The *Scivias* do not describe the visions of an
oraculating, ecstatic bride of Christ experiencing
divine union. Instead, Hildegard's prophecies are
comprised of allegorical visions followed by exege-
sis. In the excerpted passages below, which come
from Book Three of the *Scivias*, entitled "The
History of Salvation Symbolized by a Building,"
Hildegard employs the trope of the holy edifice, like
Christine de Pisan, to explore this subject. In vision
eight, Hildegard reflects on the workings of divine
grace and describes how, through grace, God draws
even the most obdurate of sinners toward
repentance.

Book 3, Vision 8: The Pillar of the Humanity of the Savior

And then I saw, on the south side of the wall of the building beyond the pillar of the true Trinity, a great and shadowed pillar, which protruded both inside and outside the building; and it was so obscure to my sight that I could not tell its size or height. And between this pillar and the pillar of the true Trinity there was a gap three cubits wide in the wall, as men-tioned above [in Vision 2, "The Edifice of Salvation"]; *only the foundation had been laid.*

Thus this shadowed pillar was standing in the same place in the building where I had previously seen, in the celestial mys-teries vouchsafed by God from above, a great four-sided radi-ance of brilliant purity. This radiance, which signifies the secrets of the supernal Creator, was shown to me in the great-est mystery; and in it, another radiance shone forth like dawn, with a deep purple light glowing in it, which was a mystical manifestation of the mystery of the incarnate Son of God. But in the pillar, there was an ascent like a ladder from bottom to top, on which I saw all the virtues of God descending and ascending, laden down with stones and going with keen zeal to their work.

And I heard that Shining One Who was seated on the throne say, *"These are God's strongest labourers!".* . . .

. . . *The first figure wore a gold crown on her head, with three higher prongs; it was radiantly adorned with green and red precious stones and white pearls. On her breast she had a shining mirror, in which appeared with wondrous brightness the image of the incarnate Son of God.* And she said:

3.8.8 Words of the Grace of God, to admonish humans

"I am the Grace of God, my little children; therefore hear and understand me, for my admonition makes radiant the souls of those who do. I keep them in blessedness, so that they will not return to iniquity. And because they have not despised me, I choose to touch them with my admonition so that they will do good works; those, that is, who seek me in simplicity and purity of heart.

"So I admonish and exhort humanity, and grant it pearls of goodness; when a person's mind is touched by me, I am his beginning. That is to say, when a person understands my admonition with his sense of hearing, and his senses consent to my touching his mind, I initiate good in him. And it is needful that he begin thus, with me helping him. Then a struggle follows: will my gift attain its end or not? How? Understand thus. When I admonish a person, so that he begins to lament and weep for his sins, then if his will consents to my admonition—for he will feel the change in his mind, and according to his mind's desire he will raise his eyes to see and his ears to hear and his mouth to speak and his hands to touch and his feet to walk—his mind will raise itself to conquer his senses, so that they will learn things their habits could not teach them . . .

"And sometimes I touch a person's mind to warn him to begin to work justice and avoid evil, but he disdains me and thinks he can do what he wants. He postpones the time of repentance until his body is reduced to old age enough to obey him, and he is so old he is tired of sinning. And then I admonish and urge him again to do good and resist in his mind. If he ignores me, he is often brought to the pass of doing good as it were unwillingly and in spite of himself, by monetary and other troubles that come upon him. And with his mind thus troubled, he has little delight in doing what he planned to do when he was prosperous and unopposed, when he thought he could act as and when he pleased. And such a person receives me in doubt; but yet I choose not to forsake him, for though it was thus he received me, he did not wholly despise me. And so I do not labor vainly in him.

"For I do not find it loathsome to touch ulcerated wounds surrounded by the filthy, gnawing worms that are innumerable vices, stinking with evil report and infamy, and stagnating in habitual wickedness. I do not refuse to close them gently up, drawing forth from them the devouring poison of malice, by touching them with the mild fire of the breath of the Holy Spirit. . . . People of little faith cannot believe it is possible for such a one to be converted to God from his iniquity; they see him as already food for the Devil. But I will not forsake this person; I choose, by my help and action, to be on his side in the struggle. . . .

"And again he looks at himself, with the same turbulence that formerly propelled him into sin; and then he turns to true repentance, with a desire as great as his former eagerness to sin. And as this person, by my warning, thus wakes from the sleep of death, which he had preferred to life, he no longer desires to sin by thought, word or deed, which before were ardently directed toward crime. And in strong repentance he rises to me; and I wholly receive him, and from henceforward discharge him as free. He will no longer be troubled by the aforesaid things, which I use to warn my dearest children to hold out against the fiery arrows of the Devil's persuasion; for he no longer needs them. For he will always sorrow at the sins he has committed, and in his self-scorn he will do such severe penance that he will deem himself unworthy to be called human. And this victory comes out of the stench of those filthy people, whom I choose not to cast out; for after sinning they have sought me . . ."

Elisabeth of Schönau
(1129–1165)

The letters below are from the Benedictine Elisabeth of Schönau to Hildegard of Bingen. Elisabeth was influenced by Hildegard's *Scivias* and had her own visionary experiences in 1152 and later. Elisabeth dictated her prophecies to her brother Ekbert, who became an abbot at the monastery at Schönau; Ekbert edited and compiled her visionary work into several volumes. She also dictated visionary letters addressed to a number of audiences. The first letter below praises Hildegard and urges her continued resistance to the heretical Cathars; when this letter was included in her book of visions, section headings were added. The second letter explains that her prophetic work is divinely mandated and asks for Hildegard's guidance and approbation regarding Elisabeth's visionary experiences. The biblical citations and bracketed explanatory notes are from the source text.

I. Rejoice with me, my lady and venerable daughter of the eternal king, since the finger of God writes in you so that you may proclaim the word of life. Blessed are you and may it be well for you forever. You are the organ of the Holy Spirit because your words enkindle me like a flame touching my heart and I burst forth in these words. [She greatly commends Hildegard and expounds to her about the leaders of the Church and the Cathars.]

My lady Hildegard, rightly are you called Hildegard because the stimulus of God works well in you with marvelous fortitude for the edification of His Church. Be strong in the Holy Spirit. Blessed are you for the Lord has chosen you and has appointed you like one of those about whom He said, "I have appointed you so that you may go and bring forth fruit and your fruit will endure" (Jn. 15:16). In this way you enter the path of contemplation of the Lord like a dove in the clefts of the rock, in the hollow in the wall (Song 2:14). The one who chose you will crown you with the crown of gladness. The way of the Lord is made straight in your presence. O lady Hildegard, carry out the work of the Lord, just as you have done so far, because the Lord has placed you as worker in His vineyard (Mt. 20:1). Indeed the Lord sought workers in His vineyard, and He found them all idle because no one leads them. The vineyard of the Lord does not have a cultivator; the vineyard of the Lord perishes; the head of the Church languishes and its members are dead. Alas, what should be done about this, since the Lord finds few in His Church who contemplate this with a blazing mind, but instead finds only those who wish to rule themselves and follow their own will. The Lord has tested them and found them sleeping. On account of this a thief has come and broken in and destroyed the foundation stone, and threw it in a cistern that had no water and was not irrigated. The foundation stone is the head of the Church which was thrown away. The Church of God is arid, having no moisture, and it is cold in love for God. But I also recall to myself that once there appeared to me poisonous serpents about to come into the Church of God, secretly hoping to destroy God's Church. I understand this to refer to those Cathars who are now secretly beguiling the church of God. Expel them, Lord, our protector! And blessed is the one who will not be scandalized in this time. The patriarch David said, "Will those who sleep not rise again?" (Ps. 40:9). Arise and be stirred and keep watch because the vengeance of God shouts

to you! Shriek, pastors, and cry aloud! Sprinkle yourselves
with ashes and repent (Jer. 25:34)! Don't give place to the
devil (Eph. 4:27), because like a roaring lion he circles, seeking what he may devour (1 Pt. 5:8). Blessed is the one who
fears the Lord of all creation and thus agitates the high priest
so that he will remove the opprobrium from his people (Is.
25:8) and all Israel will be saved. [She expounds to Hildegard
about their contempt for the Lord and His saints.]

Now, moreover, my people are perverse to me, and stiff-
necked they walk in my presence, and they do not think about
how to bear my judgment: with flagellation and making offer-
ings to myself and my saints who daily cry before my throne
saying, "Lord, king of eternal glory, in your speech all things
are ordained and there is no one who can resist your will.
Avenge our blood (Rv. 6:10), because the earth oppresses us
with their contaminations." I the Lord, creator of all creatures,
have sent my incarnate Word from the heights of the heavens
into the dark valley so that it would illuminate those who were
in shadows and who thought they were something but were
nothing. And the people loved the shadows more than the
light. But this was the true light and like the morning star in
the midst of fog (Eccl. 50:6), and like the sun shining in its
strength in the middle of the day (Rv. 1:16), so did He shine in
the midst of His people, full of wisdom and fortitude, and the
whole earth was filled with His teaching, yet you have forgotten Him. I swear by my right hand and my throne that this will
no longer be. [She turns her sermon to the people of God.]

O human, whoever you are, what reason can you use to
excuse yourself? You have eyes and you do not see, and ears
for hearing and you do not understand. What more shall I do
for you? If you lose Him, who do you think is going to redeem
you? Remember that the only Son of my heart died once for
your sins and arose and ascended into heaven and sits in His
glory and left you a model so that you could follow His footsteps. How, by what heart, or by what knowledge, do you follow Him? Far indeed are His ways from your ways. If you will

not walk like He walked, how can you come to Him? Do not
turn aside to the right or the left, but follow His footsteps and
in this way you can come to Him. But now you are slipping
from sin to sin, from damnation to damnation. Walk, while
there is light in you, lest the shadows surround you, for that
ancient leviathan thinks that he is about to swallow the whole
world. But there is still time for grace. Do penance, seek the
Lord your God while He may be found; call upon Him while
He is near (Is. 55:6). Turn to me with your whole heart, and I
the Lord will be turned to you and will be reconciled with you
and I will not abandon you in the time of tribulation and dis-
tress (2 Mc. 1:5). And that ancient serpent will fall into such a
ruin that even his guts will be poured out. [Again she speaks
about the Cathars.]

What is this that I have said about the guts of the ancient
serpent? There are some people who are now swallowed up in
his gut and later will be cast forth. They are murderers, adul-
terers, plunderers—the unjust who have hurled their souls
into death. They are also the wretched Cathars who are more
abominable than all creatures and utter their blazing words in
sulfury tongues. The earth is contaminated by their abominable faith. Just as once the peoples crucified me, so daily I
am crucified among them because they cultivate such prac-
tices. Oh what devilish insanity! They know that I am the
creator of heaven and earth and all things in them, and I see
into the depths. They tear at my wounds, dismissing the body
and blood of my sacraments, offered for the salvation of all
believers. And if they provoke me to wrath, I the Lord in my
anger will wipe out the earth and its offspring all the way to
Hell. Cease, sinners against justice! Cease this insanity! If you
do not, I will order you to be tortured beyond belief by hellish
worms without end, in sulfur and fire inextinguishable. And
there is no faculty which can comprehend this hellish punish-
ment except that great leviathan, who has stretched out and is
seducing the whole world. [She turns her sermon to those
who have undertaken to govern the Church of God; they

should destroy the various errors of the heretics in the Catholic Church.]

Lest I strike you with the sword of my mouth, I the Lord, through my right hand, order you kings and princes, bishops and abbots, priests and everyone who is in power, to use all fortitude and the catholic faith to expel and destroy all the heresies which make schisms in my Church which I gave birth to in bitterness of my soul. Oh most miserable and wretched hypocrites! In the presence of the people you appear to be pious and innocent, yet within you are full of evil inclination. Tell me how you believe in almighty God if you do not believe that all things are possible with almighty God (Mt. 19:26)! Indeed it was possible for God to send the Holy Spirit from the seat of His great majesty into the virginal womb and for the Word of His incarnation to spring forth. Do you believe that God the Father created human beings in His own image and likeness and established them in the paradise of delight so that they would work and guard it? And that ancient serpent deceived them and they fell into sin and were thrown out for their disobedience? O unhappy hypocrite: how long do you think you will remain in your sins, not believing in the Son of God who proceeds from the Father? And therefore you don't believe He was incarnate nor truly suffered, nor was buried nor resurrected, and did not ascend into heaven and will not come to judge the living and the dead.

You, however who are learned, study the books of the New Testament and remember their words and you will find great fruit. Be renewed in the Holy Spirit and revive your souls in the structure of the Church which has been sanctified in Christ Jesus and illuminated by the holy gospel and white-washed of its ancient rust. The holy Church was united with and betrothed to the celestial bridegroom, the Son of the eternal king, who washed her crimes in the Jordan so that there would be one faith, one baptism, one church, and a single dove, and one elect of Christ Jesus. Therefore you, a chosen race, a holy people, a royal priesthood, a people of

purchase (1 Pt. 2: 9) must remember the freedom with which
I have freed you from the yoke and captivity of the devil (Gal.
4:31). Indeed for sometime you were the darkness, but now
you are the light. Walk as my beloved children, the children of
light (Eph. 5:8), says your God. And again that same Truth
spoke: "My chosen vineyard, I have planted you and made
known to you every way of truth. How have you turned away,
walking not along the straight path, but after your own sins?
You seek peace according to your own will and you say, 'There
will be peace' but it is not the Son of peace and you have put
aside peace." [She delivers a sermon to them about avoiding
simony.]

So I have been driven out, and there is no place where my
feet may rest. I stand at the door and knock, and there is no
one who lets me in. My head is full of dew (Song 5:2); my bed,
in which I was hoping to rest, has been violated by various
vices. Those who enter into my sanctuary with their impurities
stain my bed with their perverse works. My pastors are
weighed down as if in a heavy sleep, and what should I do to
awaken them? I will raise up my right hand above them. I
have been patient and have waited for them from day to day,
and they have consigned me to oblivion. Indeed the Law disappears first from the priests and elders of my people (Ez.
7:26) because they seek to sell the sacrifices of my sacraments.
Those who sell, sell judgment unto themselves. And those
who buy, buy a double-edged sword.

Again with fatherly chastisements I warn my pastors who
know my secrets: "Be imitators of me and not of the devil;
there are some who do not enter my fold by the door, but
climb in by another way, through a different path, like thieves
and robbers (Jn. 10:1), thieves because of their avarice and
robbers because they lose the souls commissioned to them.
Indeed they cover their depraved works lest they be seen by
the people. On account of this, those who are reprehensible
in their own ways do not boldly speak out against every her-
esy." Again I say to you, "Know beyond doubt that as many of

the souls which you have received to govern and guard that are lost from my sheep because of your negligence, that many will I seek from your hands. At the dreadful judgment you shall render an account and all the evils which I spread over them will flow back upon you." [She makes an exhortation to those pastors of the Church.]

Now therefore be revived and think about your predecessors the apostles and the other holy doctors of the Church who did not fear the threats of the people and the scourges of the executioner, but carried my word before kings and leaders. They were beaten and suffered many torments, but they endured all on account of my name. Therefore they stand before my throne in glory and honor which no one can reckon. There they see me not in mysteries, but eye to eye, face to face, in great brightness and majesty. Blessed is the one who reads and hears the words of this text and preserves them because they are true and have been sent from my throne through my angel for the edification of many. [How to understand her earlier comment about the Cathars, "They utter their blazing words in sulphury tongues."]

While I was thinking about the meaning of the phrase which I had spoken, "They utter their blazing words in sulphury tongues," the Lord placed these words in my mouth: "The nature of sulfur is such that its flame does not ascend on high but it burns with obscurity in bitterness. This signifies heresies which so obscurely offer poisonous words from which the blackest flames come forth and ignite the hearts of the faithful and make them hesitate in the catholic faith."

II. To Lady Hildegard, venerable mistress of the brides of Christ who are in Bingen, devout prayers with all my love, from Elisabeth, humble nun. May the grace and consolation of the Most High fill you with joy, because you have had kind pity for my disquiet, as I have understood from the words of my consoler, whom you earnestly reminded of my consolation. Just as you said that it had been revealed to you about me, I truly confess that I have recently harbored in my mind a certain cloud of anxiety on account of the many senseless, untrue words of people are saying [*sic*] about me. Now the words of the public I could easily endure if also those who walk in the habit of religion would not also bitterly afflict my spirit. For they too, spurred by I don't know what goad, mock the grace of the Lord in me and do not fear to judge rashly about matters of which they are ignorant. I also hear that certain people are circulating letters of the same spirit written in my name. They declare that I have prophesied about the Judgment Day, which indeed I have never presumed to do since its coming eludes the knowledge of all mortals. But let me reveal to you the circumstance of this rumor so that you may judge whether I said or did anything presumptuous in this matter.

As you have heard from others, the Lord has magnified His mercies in me beyond what I deserved or could ever deserve in that He has deigned to frequently reveal certain celestial mysteries to me. Indeed, through His angel He has frequently indicated to me what would happen to His people in these days unless they do penance for their iniquities, and He ordered me to announce this publicly. But to avoid arrogance and not look like an author of novelties, I tried to hide these things as much as I could. Therefore, on a certain Sunday while I was in a trance, the angel of the Lord came to me in his usual way and said, "Why do you hide gold in the mud (Mt. 25:25–26)? This is the word of God which was sent to earth through your mouth not so that it would be hidden, but so that it would be made manifest for the praise and glory of our Lord and for the salvation of His people." Having said this, he lifted a whip above me and five times he struck me sharply with it, as if in great anger. Thus for three days my whole body languished from that beating. After this, he placed his finger on my mouth saying, "You will be silent until the ninth hour, at which point you will make manifest those things which the Lord has done to you." Therefore I remained mute until the ninth hour. Then I signaled to the mistress to bring to me a certain little book which I had hidden in my bed and which contained in part those things that the Lord had done to me. When I placed this in the hands of the lord abbot who had come to visit me, my tongue was loosed in these words, "Not to us, Lord, not to us, but to your name give glory" (Ps. 113B:1). After this, I also revealed certain other things to him which I had not wanted committed to writing, namely about the Lord's great vengeance which I had learned from the angel was soon to come upon the whole world. Then I most earnestly begged him to keep this conversation to himself. Instead, he ordered me to pray and to seek from the Lord an understanding about whether or not He wished me to cover with silence those things which I had told him.

When for some time I had been prostrating myself in constant prayer about this matter, during Advent, on the Feast of Saint Barbara [December 4, 1154] at first Vigils of the night, I fell into ecstasy, and the angel of the Lord stood by me saying, "Shout strongly and cry 'Alas' to all the peoples, because the whole world has been transformed into darkness. And say, 'Go! The one who formed you from the earth has called you and He says, "Do penance, for the reign of God is at hand"' (Mt. 4:17). Excited by this message, the lord abbot began to spread the word in the presence of the magistrates of the church and religious men. Some of them heard the words with reverence but some did not, instead speaking perversely about the angel who is close to me, saying that he is a mocking spirit and has been transformed into an angel of light (2 Cor. 11:14). Whence a teacher bound me through obedience to adjure him—if he should appear to me again—through the name of the Lord to reveal to me whether he was a true angel of God or not. But I thought this was presumptuous and received the order with great fear. Then one day, while I was in a trance, the angel presented himself to me in his usual way and stood in my sight. Trembling, I said to him, "I adjure you through God the Father and the Son, and the Holy Spirit, to tell me directly if you are a true angel of God and if the visions which I have seen in my trance and the things which I have heard from your mouth are true." He responded, "Know for certain that I am a true angel of God and the visions which you have seen are true and the things which you have from my mouth are true and will truly happen unless God is reconciled to the human race. And I am the one who has for so long worked with you."

After this, on the vigil of Epiphany [January 5, 1155], while I was praying, again my lord appeared to me, but he stood at a distance with his face turned away from me. Understanding his indignation, I said to him with fear, "My lord, if I annoyed you when I adjured you, do not, I beseech, blame me. I beg you: turn your face to me and be merciful, since I was bound by obedience to act and I did not dare transgress the command of my instructor." After I had poured out many tears with words like this, he turned to me and said, "You have acted contemptibly toward me and my brothers by your lack of trust in me. From now on, know for certain that you will no longer see my face nor hear my voice unless you placate the Lord and us." I said, "My lord, how can you be placated?" He said, "Tell your abbot to celebrate devoutly the divine office in memory of me and my brothers." So when the solemnity of the Mass had been celebrated for the honor of the holy angels, not once but many times by the lord abbot as well as by the other brothers, and likewise when the sisters had honored them by reading psalms, my lord again appeared to me with a calm face and said to me, "I know that you acted in charity and obedience. For this reason you have found mercy and from now on I will visit you more frequently than before."

After this, the lord abbot arranged to go to a certain place at the request of the clergy staying there. He was to preach the Lord's word of warning to the people so that perhaps they might do penance and avert the wrath of God from themselves. But first he set about to pray to the Lord, together with all of us, that He might deign to reveal to His handmaid whether or not that sermon which he had already begun to

make public should be further divulged. While he was cele-
brating the divine mystery and we were most devoutly praying, suddenly the joints of all my limbs were loosened and I
languished and went into a trance. And behold the angel of
the Lord stood in my sight and I said to him, "My lord,
remember what you said to me your handmaid, that the word
of God was sent to earth through my mouth not so that it
could be hidden but so that it would be made known for the
glory of God and for the salvation of His people. Tell me now
what should be done about that word of warning which you
have spoken to me. Has it been made sufficiently known or
should it still be preached?" Looking at me with a severe
expression he said, "Do not test God; indeed, those who test
God shall perish. And say to the abbot, 'Do not fear, but finish
what you have begun. Truly blessed are those who hear the
words of your exhortation and keep them and are not scandalized by you.' Moreover, advise him not to change the form
which he has used so far in his preaching. Indeed, in this I
have been his counselor. Tell him that he should in no way pay
attention to the words of those who, out of envy, speak with
doubt about the things which were done to you. Rather, he
should attend to what is written, that nothing is impossible
with God" (Mt. 19:26).

Encouraged by this speech, the abbot went to the place
which he had planned to visit. He exhorted the people, who
were awaiting his arrival, to do repentance, announcing the
wrath of God about to come upon them unless they tried to
prevent it by works of penance. In some of his preaching he
did describe what kind of plagues were threatening the earth,
but not at all as he was said to have done. Therefore many
people among whom that sermon was proclaimed afflicted
themselves with penance in great fear throughout the whole
time of Lent, and zealously persevered in almsgiving and
prayers. At that time someone, led by I don't know what zeal,
sent letters to the city of Cologne in the name of the lord
abbot, although—God knows—he was ignorant of it. In these

letters, certain terrible threats were read with everybody listening. Whence although it may have been a joke from our own foolish ones, nevertheless, prudent people, so we have heard, reverently heeded the sermon and did not disdain to honor God with works of penance.

It happened moreover that on the Wednesday before Easter, when I came into ecstasy with great bodily struggle, the angel of the Lord appeared to me. I said to him, "Lord, what will be done about that message which you spoke to me?" He responded, "Do not be sad or disturbed if the things I predicted do not come to pass on the day I had indicated to you, because the Lord has been appeased by the amends made by many." On Friday after this, around the third hour, I went into a trance with severe pain. Again the angel stood by me and said, "The Lord has seen the affliction of His people, and has turned the wrath of His indignation from them." I said to him, "But then, my lord, won't I be scorned by everyone to whom this message was revealed?" He said, "You must endure patiently and with good will everything that will happen to you on this occasion. Take diligent heed of that One who, although He was the creator of the whole world, endured the mockeries of human beings. Now the Lord is testing your patience for the first time."

Behold, my lady, I have explained to you the whole order of the affair so that you may know the innocence of both myself and our abbot, and so that you can make it known to others. I beg you, moreover, to make me a partner in your prayers, and that as soon as the Spirit of the Lord prompts you, write back to me with some words of consolation.

Beatrijs of Nazareth
(c. 1200–1268)

Beatrijs came from a religious family (her father had founded three religious houses) and was highly educated in the liberal arts. Beatrijs first received instruction in a Beguine community. The Beguines were laywomen who formed religious communities that were not affiliated with a specific order or even sanctioned by the church, though some communities might look to nearby monastic orders for spiritual guidance. After studying with the Beguines, Beatrijs received further instruction at abbeys. She became the prioress of the convent at Nazareth, where she composed her *Seven Manners*. Though Beatrijs was not a Beguine herself, she describes the soul's union with the divine in terms similar to Mechthild's or Hadewijch's; however, *Seven Manners* focuses not on Beatrijs's own personal experiences of divine ecstasy, but rather on the paths and characteristics of spiritual loving open to all souls. Compare Beatrijs's message of love to that of Thérèse of Lisieux in this volume.

There Are Seven Manners of Loving

4. In the fourth manner of loving, it is our Lord's custom to give sometimes great joy, sometimes great woe; and let us now speak of this.

Sometimes it happens that love is sweetly awakened in the soul and joyfully arises and stirs itself in the heart without

any help from human acts. And then the heart is so tenderly
touched in love, so powerfully assailed, so wholly encom-
passed and so lovingly embraced in love that the soul is
altogether conquered by love. Then it feels a great closeness
to God and a spiritual brightness and a wonderful richness
and a noble freedom and a great compulsion of violent love,
and an overflowing fullness of great delight. And then the
soul feels that all its senses and its will have become love,
that it has sunk down so deeply and been engulfed so completely in love, that it has entirely become love. Love's
beauty has adorned the soul, love's power has consumed it,
love's sweetness has submerged it, love's righteousness has
engulfed it, love's excellence has embraced it, love's purity
has enhanced it, love's exaltedness has drawn it up and
enclosed it, so that the soul must be nothing else but love
and do nothing else.

When the soul feels itself to be thus filled full of riches and
in such fullness of heart, the spirit sinks away down into love,
the body seems to pass away, the heart to melt, every faculty
to fail; and the soul is so utterly conquered by love that it often
cannot support itself, often the limbs and the senses lose their
powers. And just as a vessel filled up to the brim will run over
and spill if it is touched, so at times the soul is so touched and
over-powered by this great fullness of the heart that in spite of
itself it spills and overflows.

5. In the fifth manner, it also sometimes happens that love is
powerfully strengthened in the soul and rises violently up, with
great tumult and force, as if it would break the heart with its
assault and drag the soul out of itself in the exercise and the
delight of love. And then the soul is drawn in the longing of love
to fulfill the great and pure deeds of love and the desires
implanted by love's many promptings. Or sometimes the soul
longs to rest in the sweet embrace of love, in that desirable state
of richness and satisfaction which comes from the possession of
love, so that the heart and all the senses long and seek eagerly

and long wholly for this. When the soul is in this state, it is so strong in spirit, so open in heart to receive all things, so strong in bodily power to do all things, more able to accomplish its works, achieving so much, that it seems to the soul itself that there is nothing which it cannot do and perform, even though in the body it were to remain idle. At the same time the soul feels itself so greatly stirred from within, such an utter dependence upon love, such an impatient desire for love and the countless sorrows of a deep dissatisfaction. And sometimes when the soul experiences love that brings it woe without it ever knowing why, or it may be because it is so stirred to long for love, or because it is filled with dissatisfaction that it cannot know love's full delight.

And at times love becomes so boundless and so overflowing in the soul, when it itself is so mightily and violently moved in the heart, that it seems to the soul that the heart is wounded again and again, and that these wounds increase every day in bitter pain and in fresh intensity. It seems to the soul that the veins are bursting, the blood spilling, the marrow withering, the bones softening, the heart burning, the throat parching, so that the body in its every part feels this inward heat, and this is the fever of love. Sometimes the soul feels that the whole body is transfixed, and it is as if every sense would fail; and like a devouring fire, seizing upon everything and consuming everything which it can master, love seems to be working violently in the soul, relentless, uncontrollable, drawing everything into it and devouring it.

All this torments and afflicts the soul, and the heart grows sick and the powers dwindle; yet it is so that the soul is fed and love is fostered and the spirit is subjected to love.

For love is exalted to high above the soul's comprehension, above all that the soul can do or suffer, that even though at such times it may long to break the bond that unites it to love, that cannot harm love's singleness; and the soul is so fettered with the bond of love, so conquered by the boundlessness of love, that it cannot rule itself by reason, cannot reason through understanding, cannot spare itself this weariness, cannot hold fast to human wisdom.

For the more there is given from above to the soul, the more is demanded of it: the more is revealed to the soul, the more it is filled with longing to come close to the light of that truth, that purity, that excellence and that delight which are love's attributes. Always the soul will be driven and goaded on, never will it be satisfied and at rest. For what most afflicts and torments the soul is that which most heals and assuages it; what gives the soul its deepest wounds bring to it best relief.

6. In the sixth manner, as the bride of our Lord advances and climbs into greater holiness, she feels love to be of a different nature, and her knowledge of this love is closer and higher.

The soul feels that love has conquered its every shortcoming, and has mastered the senses and adorned its humanity, and increased and exalted its being, and has utterly overpowered it without any resistance, so that the heart is made steadfast in confidence, and can freely practice all the exercises of love and delight in love and take its rest. When the soul is in this state, there is nothing which it must perform or abandon, suffer and endure, which does not seem to it petty and easy, for this is one of love's noble qualities, and so it is easy for the soul to busy itself in the exercises of love.

Then the soul feels in itself a closeness to God which comes from Him, a radiant purity, a sweetness of the spirit, a loving freedom, a savoring wisdom, a gentle drawing near to our Lord and a close comprehension of God.

And you may see that now the soul is like a housewife who has put all her household in good order and prudently arranged it and well disposed it: she has taken good care that nothing will damage it, her provision for the future is wise, she knows exactly what she is doing, she acquires and discards, she does what is proper, she avoids mistakes, and always she knows how everything should be. So it is with the soul: the soul is all love, and love rules in the soul, mighty and powerful, working and resting, doing and not doing, and all which is in the soul and comes to the soul is according to love's will.

And like the fish, swimming in the vast sea and resting in its deeps, and like the bird, boldly mounting high in the sky, so the soul feels its spirit freely moving through the vastness and the depth and the unutterable richness of love.

It is love's power which has seized the soul and led it, sheltered and protected it, given it prudence and wisdom and the sweetness and the strength which belong to love. Yet still at this time love hides from the soul its own power, that it has mounted to greater heights and that it is master of itself and that it is love which reigns triumphantly in it. And then love makes the soul so bold that it no longer fears man nor friend, angel or saint or God Himself in all that it does or abandons, in all its working and resting. And now the soul feels indeed that love is within it, as mighty and as active when the body is at rest as when it performs many deeds.

The soul knows well and feels that love is not found in the labor and suffering of those in whom it rules, but that all who want to attain to love must seek it in fear and pursue it in faith, exercising themselves in longing, not sparing themselves in great labors, in many sufferings, undergoing many sorrows and enduring much contempt. The soul must not despise these things: small though they be, they must seem great, until it attains to the state where love rules in it and performs its own mighty works, making great things small, labor easy, suffering sweet, and all debts paid.

This is freedom of conscience, sweetness of heart, subjection of the senses, the soul's excellence, the spirit's exaltation, and the beginning of everlasting life. This is to live the life of angels here in the flesh, that everlasting life which may God grant to us all. Amen.

Mechthild of Magdeburg
(c. 1207–c. 1282)

An educated young woman, Mechthild joined a Beguine community at Magdeburg, where she remained until late in her life, when she joined a Cistercian monastery at Helfta. This Beguine community received spiritual guidance from the Dominicans, and Mechthild was apparently encouraged by her confessor to record her prophetic experiences and inspired writings. *The Flowing Light of the Godhead* combines writings from many years. Books 1–6 were written while Mechthild was still among the Beguines, while Book 7 was composed after she had moved to the convent at Helfta. The text includes writings of various genres, including poetry, dramatic dialogues, and prose, which draw on tropes of courtly love poetry as well as the Song of Songs.

This is the first part of the book.

This book is to be joyfully welcomed for God Himself speaks in it. This book I now send forth as a messenger to all spiritual people both good and bad—for if the pillars fall, the building cannot stand. The book proclaims Me alone and shows forth My holiness with praise. All who would understand this book should read it nine times.

This book is called The Flowing Light of the Godhead. Ah! Lord God! Who has written this book? I in my weakness have written it, because I dared not hide the gift that is in it.

Ah! Lord! What shall this book be called to Thy Glory! It shall be called *The Flowing Light of My Godhead* into all hearts which dwell therein without falseness.

1. *How Love and the Soul, who sits enthroned as Queen, speak together.*

Soul:
God greet thee Lady, thy name
Is known to me, it is Love.

Love:
God reward thee, O Queen!

Soul:
Love! I am happy to meet thee!

Love:
And I by the greeting, much honored.

Soul:
Love, thou didst wrestle long years
With the Holy Trinity
Till the overflow fell once for all
In Mary's humble lap!

Love:
But, O Queen, these things were done
For thy honor and thy delight.

Soul:
Ah Love! thou hast taken from me
All I had won on earth!

Love:
A blessed exchange, O Queen!

Soul:
To deprive me of my childhood?

Love:
In exchange for heavenly freedom!

Soul:
Thou hast taken away my youth!

Love:
In exchange for many virtues.

Soul:
Thou hast taken my friends and relations!

Love:
Queen! that is a false charge!

Soul:
And taken from me the world,
Honor and all my possessions!

Love:
These all I shall, O Queen,
In one hour by as much as thou wilt
Of the Holy Spirit, make good to thee.

Soul:
Love, thou hast tried me so sore
Through suffering, that now my body
Can barely support its weight.

Love:
Against that loss, O Queen,
Thou hast gained great understanding.

Soul:
Ah! Love! thou hast consumed
My very flesh and blood!

Love:
Thereby art thou enlightened
And raised up to God.

Soul:
But Love, thou art a robber,
Make thou that good to me!

Love:
That will I do, O Queen,
I pray thee—take myself!

Soul:
Now even here on earth
Thou'st paid me back again
A hundred-fold, O Love!

Love:
My Queen, now God and all
His heavenly realm, are thine.

4. *Of the presence at Court of the soul to whom God shows Himself.* When the poor soul comes to Court, she is discreet and modest. She looks at her God with joyful eyes. Ah! how lovingly she is there received! She is silent but longs above everything to praise Him. And He, with great desire, shows her His Divine heart. It glows like red gold in a great fire. And God lays the soul in His glowing heart so that He, the great God, and she, the humble maid, embrace and are as one as water with wine. Then she is overcome and beside herself for weakness and can no more. And He is overpowered with love for her, as He ever was, He neither gives nor takes. Then she says, "Lord! Thou art my Beloved! My desire! My flowing stream! My Sun! And I am thy reflection!"

Thus does the loving soul who cannot exist without God, come to Court.

21. *Of Knowledge and Revelation.*

Love without Knowledge
Is darkness to the wise soul.
Knowledge without revelation

Is as the pain of Hell.
Revelation without death,
Cannot be endured.

26. *In this way the soul leads the senses and is free and without grief.* It is a wondrous and lofty way in which the faithful
soul walks, leading the senses after it as a man with sight might
lead one who was blind. In this way the soul is free and travels
without grief in its heart, seeing that it wills nothing but what
its Lord wills Who does everything for the best.

27. *How thou art to become worthy of the Way, to walk in it
and be perfected.* Three things make the soul worthy of this
way so that it recognizes it and walks in it. Firstly, that it wills
to come to God, renouncing all self-will, joyfully welcoming
God's grace and willingly accepting all its demands against
human desires. The second thing which keeps the soul in the
way is that all things are welcome to it save sin alone. The
third thing makes the creature perfect in the way, namely, that
it does all things to the glory of God, so that even its smallest
desire will be as highly prized by God as if it were in the highest state of contemplation possible to humanity.

For all is done in love to the glory of God. Therefore all is one.
But if I sin, then I am no longer in this way!

38. *God rejoices that the soul has overcome four sins.*

Our Lord delights in Heaven
Because of the loving soul He has on earth,
And says, "Look how she who was wounded
    Me [*sic*] has risen!
She has cast from her the apes of worldliness;
Overcome the bear of impurity,
Trodden the lion of pride underfoot,
Torn the wolf of desire from his revenge,
And comes racing like a hunted deer

To the spring which is Myself.
She comes soaring like an eagle
Swinging herself from the depths
Up into the heights."

Hadewijch of Brabant
(c. early to mid-1200s)

The historical record tells us little about Hadewijch of Brabant. She was a Beguine mystic, like Mechthild of Magdeburg, and she was highly educated, judging by the range of knowledge displayed in her writings. She may have founded or led a Beguine community, or she may have just been part of one. Her work includes letters, visions, and poems in stanzas and various forms. The following pages contain a Letter to a Young Beguine, offering a brief autobiographical spiritual narrative that describes the paradox of Hadewijch's experience of loving God, as well as one of her visions.

Letter 11. Ah, dear child, may God give you what my heart longs that you should have: and that would be for you to love God as He deserves. And yet, dear child, I have never been able to endure the thought that anyone before me could have loved Him so dearly as I. Yet of course I believe that there were many who have loved Him as much and as dearly, even though I could not suffer to think that anyone could have known Him or loved Him so greatly as I.

Since I was ten years old, I have been so possessed by a wholehearted loved for God that in the first two years when I began to love Him so, I should have died, had He not given me greater strength than most people have, and given to my nature the power of His nature; and often He gave me counsel, which sometimes was illumined with many gracious

49

shewings; and I received from Him many wonderful gifts in which I felt and I saw what He is. And in all these tokens of love which I felt between Him and me, according to the usages of love, just as lovers use between themselves, concealing little, giving much, finding most in their close communion one with another, each one as it were tasting all, eating all, drinking all, consuming all the other, in all these tokens which God my Love so plentifully gave to me at the beginning of my life, He gave me trust in Him, that from then on I generally felt that no one had loved Him with so whole a heart as I. But there were times when reason said indeed to me that I was not the one who loved Him best. But though I thought this, I could never feel it or believe it, so closely was I bound to Him in the bonds of true Love.

So this is how I am now: in the end, I cannot believe that I have loved Him best, and yet I cannot believe that there is any living man who loved God as I love Him. So sometimes Love illumines me so that I know how far short I fall, that I am not enough for my Love, that I do not love Him as He deserves; and at times the sweet nature of Love grants me so to taste and to feel Love that I am blinded, that that suffices me, that I am so rich in being together with Love that I confess to Love that Love alone suffices me.

Vision 10. *The Bride in the City.* I was taken up in the spirit on the feast of Saint John the Evangelist in the Christmas Octave. There I saw prepared a new city of the same name as Jerusalem and of the same appearance. It was being adorned with all sorts of new ornaments (cf. Apoc. 21:2) that were unspeakably beautiful. They who served in the city were the most beautiful of heaven, and all belonged among those called Auriolas and Eunustus. And all who had been sanctified by Love, together with all the living, adorned it and evoked all the new wonders that gave rise to new admiration. And in the midst of the high city flew an eagle crying with a loud voice: "All you lords and wielders of power, here shall you learn the eternity of your domain!" And he flew a second time through the city, crying: "The time is at hand! All you living, find joy in her who possesses the true life!"

And a third time he cried and said: "O you dead, come into the light and into the life! And all you who are unready, insofar as you are not too naked to attend our marriage (cf. Matt. 22:1–14), come to our abundance and contemplate the bride, who by love has experienced all needs, heavenly and earthly! She is so experienced with need in the alien land that I shall now show her how she has grown in the *land of darkness* (Job 10:33). And she shall be great, and she shall see her repose, and the voice of power shall be wholly hers."

After this an Evangelist came and said: "You are here, and you shall be shown the glory of your exile. The city you here see adorned is your free conscience; and the lofty beauty that is here is your manifold virtues with full suffering; and the adornment is your fiery ardor, which remains dominant in you in spite of all disasters. Your unknown virtues with new assiduity are the manifold ornaments that adorn the city. Your blessed soul is the bride in the city. Here is that highest society which wholly lives in love and in the spirit of the highest virtue. All those whom you see here, Eunustus and Auriolas, and the whole multitude who are highest in power, have come here to participate in your marriage. Moreover all the living, both of heaven and earth, shall renew their life in this marriage. The dead sinners—who have come without hope, and are enlightened by the knowledge of your union, and desire grace or entrance into purgatory—cling somewhat to virtue and are not altogether naked. If only they believe in the oneness of you both, they will find full contentment through your marriage."

Then I heard a Voice loudly crying: "New peace be to all of you, and all new joy! Behold, this is my bride, who has passed through all your honors with perfect love, and whose love is so strong that, through it, all attain growth!" And he said, "Behold, Bride and Mother, you like no other have been able to live [*sic*] me as God and Man! What do you think they who are Eunustus to all earthly repose become? That is what you are for all of them collectively. You alone have never tasted earthly poison; you like no other have superhumanly suffered much among men. You shall suffer everything to the end with which I am, and we shall remain one. Now enjoy fruition of me, what I am, with the strength of your victory, and they shall live eternally contented through you."

The Voice embraced me with an unheard of wonder, and I swooned in it, and my spirit failed me to see or hear more. And I lay in this fruition half an hour, but then the night was over, and I came back, piteously lamenting my exile, as I have done all this winter. For truly the whole winter long I have been occupied with this kind of thing. I lay there a long time and possessed love, or revelations, or anything else in particular that Love gave me.

Angela of Foligno
(c. 1248–1309)

Angela was born in Foligno, married at a young age and had children, and was purportedly a worldly young woman. After experiencing a crisis of conscience, she had a vision of Saint Francis of Assisi. She became a Franciscan tertiary, a member of a lay order, and told her conversion narrative to the Franciscan Friar Arnaldo, who served as her confessor and as editor of her first book. Her visionary experiences and explication of doctrine are included in her *Book of Divine Consolation*. She was an important figure for the Franciscans, and helped to gather a large community of men and women into the lay Third Order. The chapters below come from the second treatise in her *Libro*. Angela draws upon the language and imagery of the Song of Songs to expound upon the experiences of the soul's union with God.

Treatise II, Chapter XXIX. *Of the Various Properties of Love.* In order to understand how the aforesaid wisdom ruleth the love of God, ye must know that love hath various properties. Firstly, it maketh tender; secondly, it maketh sick; and thirdly, it maketh strong.

When the soul feeleth divine love it crieth aloud and maketh a noise like unto a stone which is placed in a furnace to be turned into lime. If the stone be touched by the fire it cracketh noisily, but if it be baked it maketh no noise. Thus the soul doth in the beginning seek divine consolation, but when it hath been overwhelmed thereby, it groweth weak and crieth out against God, lamenting and saying, "Lord, why hast Thou sent this weakness upon me?"

Great audacity, however, is born of that assurance which the soul hath of God. It knoweth of a certainty that God loveth it deeply and doth sometimes favor it by giving it marvellous and ineffable consolations; but these must not be demanded with importunity. Nevertheless, if God giveth them they are not to be refused, for they draw the soul nigh unto the beloved, they are its food, they do cure its weariness, and through them is it uplifted and drawn unto seeking, loving, and being united with its beloved.

In this state is the soul contented with consolations, but through the deprivation thereof doth love increase and begin to seek for the beloved. And when it findeth him not it falleth sick and is no more contented with consolations, because it seeketh its beloved alone. And the more consolation, knowledge, and other such things that it hath, the more doth love increase, and the more sick and weary doth it become if it be not in the presence of its beloved.

But when the soul is united and placed in the seat of truth, which truth is the seat of the soul, it crieth no more, neither doth it murmur against God; it groweth no more weak, nor falleth sick, but is filled with marvellous wisdom and ripeness and becometh stable and orderly, and is so strengthened that for love of its beloved would it go even unto death, inasmuch as it possesseth in abundance the qualities needful for that union.

And God Himself maketh the soul to grow, in order that it may hold all that which He desireth to put into it. And the soul beholdeth this thing, and perceiveth that all other things are as nothing if they come not from this.

Then the soul esteemeth as nothing all that it had been heretofore in comparison with what it is now; it regardeth not anything created, it careth neither for death nor infirmity, neither for honour nor disgrace, and so peaceful and full of comfort is it that nothing can rouse it; it hath lost all desire and it cannot work, for when it seeth the aforesaid visions it can do nothing whatever.

Thus it appeareth that God doeth all things according to His wisdom and in an orderly and seemly manner; for we fall not sick even when He is absent, and thus do we conform unto His will. Although He be absent we seek Him not, but are satisfied with what He hath ordained and trust wholly in Him.

But when these visions are withdrawn from the soul (because none are allowed in this present life to continue therein), there is given and doth remain unto it a new and ardent desire to perform without trouble the works of penitence more vigorously than heretofore, and assuredly this state is more sublime than was the other.

And the love now kindled is perfect and causeth the loving soul to imitate its Beloved, Christ crucified, whose sufferings did endure all the time that He lived this mortal life. Thus He began, continued, and ended; He was ever upon the Cross of poverty, grief, contempt, and obedience, and all the other hard deeds of penitence. Whosoever loveth another perfectly useth all his endeavor to make himself one with that person, following his example and doing those things which please him. Likewise whosoever loveth Jesus, God and Man, will endeavor to transform himself in Him, following His example and doing that which he believeth will please Him, and in his manner of life seeking to be as like unto Him as possible.

Chapter XXX. *The More Perfect Man is, the More Earnestly Doth He Endeavor to Do That Which is Desired, Ordered, and Counseled of God.* The more perfect a man is and the more he loveth God, the more doth he strive to do these things which God did, which He desireth, commandeth, and counseleth should be done, and to avoid those things which displease Him. And he must do this all the days of his life, for when the Man of Sorrows lived this mortal life He was ever upon a bitter cross of penitence. The length of time, therefore, ordained for penance, is as long as a man shall live. The amount and severity thereof must be according as a man can with discretion perform. And this is unity with the will of God, a unity which He hath ordained should not be only in words, but in doing the works of the Cross and of penitence, such as Christ Himself performed.

When the soul is transformed in God and is in God, and hath that perfect union and fullness of vision, it is quiet and worketh nothing whatsoever. But when it cometh again to itself it striveth to transform itself in the will of God in order that it may behold again that vision wherewith it directeth the love of God and of its neighbor as though with arms. For herein doth the soul behold the Being of God, and how all creatures have their being from that Supreme Being, and it perceiveth that there existeth nothing which doth not derive its being from that same Supreme Being.

From this vision doth the soul, thus instructed, draw marvelous learning, ineffable wisdom, and ripe gravity, and from this vision it draweth likewise the true knowledge of the perfection of all things appertaining unto that Supreme Being; and it cannot doubt it, for it perceiveth how that all things made by Him are well made. Bad are they only when we ourselves destroy what the Supreme Being hath made well.

This vision of the Supreme Being awakeneth a love corresponding unto itself. The Supreme Being inciteth us to love everything which hath its being from Him, all good things and well made things, and teacheth us to love all creatures, rational and irrational, for love of Him; and everything, whatsoever it may be, which hath its being from Him and which He loveth, doth He incite us also to love. Especially doth He teach us to love those creatures in which we perceive He taketh an especial delight; for when the soul findeth that Supreme Being yearneth in love towards His creatures, then will it also yearn towards them.

The sign manifest of those who stand in the friendship of the Supreme Being is, that they are true followers of His only

Son, that they keep the eyes of their mind ever fixed upon Him, ready to love and follow Him, and in all things to transform themselves in the will of the Beloved, namely, the only begotten Son of the Supreme Being.

Chapter XXXIII. *The Way To Find the Love of God is By Constant, Untiring, Devout and Ardent Prayer, and The Reading of the Book of Life.* The way unto this love is by constant, assiduous, devout and ardent prayer, and the reading of the Book of Life, of which much hath already been said, and whence we obtain that knowledge of God which it is needful for us to have if we would also have His love, as hath already been set forth.

Oh my beloved, take comfort, and see that we love God and wholly transform ourselves in Him; for this Christ, God uncreate, God incarnate, is all love, and therefore loveth all and desireth to be wholly loved. Wherefore doth He desire that His children should be wholly transformed in Him through love.

I pray you, oh ye spiritual children, chosen through love, ye who live in the grace and charity of the good and perfect God, I pray you transform yourselves with the perfection of love. True is it that we are all sons of God by creation, but His elect spiritual children are they in whom the God of love hath planted His love and in whom He delighteth, because He findeth His own likeness in them, which likeness in the soul of each one of the sons of God is formed there solely through the grace of God and the perfect love divine. And perfect is he who hath already transformed his manners and life in the likeness of the life of Christ, who lived in this world poor and despised and full of suffering.

God, therefore, whose nature is noble, desireth to possess the whole heart of His son and not only a part thereof, and He desireth it immediately, and without companionship or hindrance or anything contrary whatsoever. But He is so merciful unto the soul that if it giveth Him its whole heart He accepteth it willingly, and if it giveth Him only a part He accepteth also the part, albeit His perfect love longeth naturally for the whole and not only a part.

We know that the bridegroom who loveth his bride cannot endure that she should have any other companion either openly or in secret. In like manner cannot God endure it. But well do I know that if any person were to understand and taste of that divine love of God who was made man and crucified for us and who is the Supreme Good, he would give himself wholly unto Him, he would take himself away not only from other creatures, but also from his own self, and would love this loving God with his whole heart, and transform himself entirely in God, the Supreme Love.

Wherefore, if the soul desireth to attain unto this perfection of perfect love, which giveth itself wholly and doth not serve God for sake of the reward which it hopeth to receive from Him, or because of the future life, but giveth itself unto God and serveth Him for His own sake, who is essentially good in Himself and worthy of being loved for Himself, then the soul must enter by the straight way and must walk thereon with the feet of pure love, upright, fervent, and orderly.

But the first step to be taken by the soul who entereth upon this straight way and desireth to draw nigh unto God is to learn to know God in very truth, and not only outwardly, as though by the color of the writing (as hath been already said). For as we know so do we love; therefore if we know but little and darkly, if we do reflect and meditate upon Him only superficially and fleetingly, we shall in consequence love Him but little, as hath been said afore.

Chapter XXXIV. *Of the Properties of Lovers.* There are three properties peculiar unto lovers of which it is needful to know. Likewise certain signs of love, whereby each may know whether he be a true lover or not.

The first property is to be truly transformed in the will of the Beloved. To me it seemeth that His will is His life, which

He showeth forth in His own self; herein doth He show us poverty, suffering, and contempt, which we must all experience indeed, and when the soul is strengthened and practiced in these things neither vice nor temptation can enter into it.

The second property is to be transformed in the properties of the Beloved, of which I will at present mention three only. The first is love; that is, to love all creatures according as is seemly. The second is to be humble and gentle. The third (which is given by God unto His lawful children) is steadfastness; for the nearer the soul is unto God, the less doth it change in its own self. We are ashamed when we are moved by anything vile, and herein know we our great wretchedness.

The third property is to be wholly transformed in God, and then we are beyond all temptation. Then do we no longer live in ourselves, but in Him; but when we fall back again into our misery we do beware of all creatures and of our own selves.

I pray you, keep control over yourselves and give not yourselves unto any creature, neither lend yourselves unto aught whatsoever; but give yourselves wholly unto Him who saith, "Thou shalt love the Lord with all thine heart, and with all thy mind, and with all thy soul, and with all the strength that thou hast."

Of the Signs of Love. These are the signs of love.

The first sign of true love is that the lover submitteth his own will unto the will of the beloved. The second is that he forsaketh all other friendship which might be contrary unto his love. He likewise forsaketh father and mother, brother and sister, and all other affection which is contrary unto the will of the beloved.

The third is, that there is nothing hidden in one which is not revealed unto the other; and this (according unto my thinking) is the sum and complement of all the other signs and workings of love.

The fourth and last is, that the lover doth strive to make himself like unto the beloved. If the beloved be poor, he striveth to be poor; if the beloved be reputed vile, then he seeketh to be vile also; if the beloved be in grief, he seeketh to be a sharer of that woe, in order that the condition of one may be like unto that of the other.

Of a truth I do hold that true and perfect love cannot exist betwixt rich and poor, honorable and vile, sorrowful and joyous, because these conditions are widely different one from another, and there can be no perfect love betwixt them because one doth not share the condition of the other. Love is a true virtue, which not only maketh things like unto each other but also uniteth them, and it always leadeth the soul unto its like and not unto its opposite.

Of a certainty did Jesus Christ, the Eternal Love, possess all these signs. He submitted His will unto man's will, and even unto death was He obedient unto those who slew Him, albeit He could have overthrown them by only raising His hand. Moreover He forsook all friendship, His kindred and His mother and His own flesh and blood for man's sake, leaving them and going to His death upon the Cross. He did also reveal unto us His secrets, saying, "I have not called you servants," &c. Moreover, He desired to make Himself like unto man, taking upon Himself true humanity and mortality, becoming like unto man in all things, saving only sin.

Therefore ought we also to do all these things for His sake; otherwise love goeth halting upon our side, and doth great wrong unto that passionate Lover. Wherefore let us make ourselves like unto Him in all things (in which He made Himself like unto our wretchedness), doing penance in that poverty, contempt, pain, and contrition of heart in which He always lived. Of a truth, if one person alone were to perform all the acts of penance which are performed by all the men in the world, they would not suffice to repay the smallest drop of sweat which Christ shed for us, nor would they be enough to merit the least of the joys of Paradise promised unto us, nor to give satisfaction for the least of the mortal sins by us committed, nor yet to repay God for our creation.

Gertrude the Great
(1256–1302)

When she was just a child, Saint Gertrude entered the same convent at Helfta where Mechthild of Magdeburg spent the last years of her life (Mechthild would have arrived there when Gertrude was an adolescent). Her intellectual and spiritual development at Helfta is described in both a biography, written by another sister, and a spiritual autobiography. Elizabeth Petroff suggests that it was Mechthild's presence that made Helfta an atmosphere in which women's writing was encouraged. In the passage below, Gertrude reflects on the divine mandate that she spread God's message through her writings and shares her experiences of intimate communication with God.

Chapter X. *How the Lord obliged her to write these things; and how He illuminated her.* I considered it so unsuitable for me to publish these writings, that my conscience would not consent to do so; therefore I deferred doing it until the Feast of the Exaltation of the Holy Cross.[1] On that day, having determined before Mass to apply myself to other occupations, the Lord conquered the repugnance of my reason by these words: "Be assured that you will not be released from the prison of the flesh until you have paid this debt which still binds you." And as I reflected that I had already employed the gifts of God for the advancement of my neighbor if not by my

---

[1] September 14. [Note in source text.]

writing, at least by my words He brought forward these words which I had heard used at the preceding Matins: "If the Lord had willed to teach His doctrine only to those who were present, He would have taught by word only, not by writing. But now they are written for the salvation of many." He added further: "I desire your writings to be an indisputable evidence of My Divine goodness in these latter times, in which I purpose to do good to many."

These words having depressed me, I began to consider within myself how difficult and even impossible it would be to find thoughts and words capable of explaining these things to the human intellect without scandal. But the Lord delivered me from this pusillanimity by pouring out on my soul an abundant rain, the impetuous fall of which weighed me down like a young and tender plant vile creature that I am! instead of watering me gently, so as to make me increase in perfection; and I could find no profit from it, except from some weighty words, the sense of which I was unable perfectly to penetrate. Therefore, finding myself still more depressed, I inquired what would be the advantage of these writings; and Thy goodness, my God, solaced my trouble with Thy usual sweetness, refreshing my soul by this reply: "Since this deluge appears useless to you, behold, I will now approach you to My Divine Heart, that your words may be gentle and sweet, according to the capabilities of your mind." Which promise, my Lord and my God, Thou didst most faithfully fulfill. And for four days, at a convenient hour each morning, Thou didst suggest with so much clearness and sweetness what I composed, that I have been able to write it without difficulty and without reflection, even as if I had learned it by heart long before; with this limitation, that when I had written a sufficient quantity each day, it has not been possible for me, although I applied my whole mind to it, to find a single word to express the things which on the following day I could write freely: thus instructing and refraining my impetuosity, as the Scripture teaches: "Let none so apply himself to action as to omit contemplation." Thus art

Thou jealous for my welfare; and whilst Thou givest me leisure to enjoy the embraces of Rachel, Thou dost not permit me to be deprived of the glorious fruitfulness of Lia. May Thy wise love deign to accomplish in me these two things!

Chapter XIX. *How God is pleased to condescend to His creatures; and what glory God derives thence from the blessed.* I give thanks to Thy loving mercy and to Thy merciful love, most loving Lord, for the revelation by which Thy goodness satisfied my weak and wavering soul when I so ardently desired to be released from the chains of the flesh: not that I might suffer less, but that I might release Thy goodness from the debt which Thy exceeding love has undertaken for my salvation; although Thy Divine omnipotence and eternal wisdom were not obliged to grant me this favor, but Thou didst bestow it on my unworthiness and ingratitude of Thy super abounding liberality.

When, therefore, I desired to be dissolved, Thou, my God, who art the honor and glory of heaven, didst appear to me, descending from the royal throne of Thy majesty, and approaching to sinners by a most obliging and favorable condescension; and then certain streams of precious liquor seemed to flow through heaven, before which all the saints prostrated themselves in thanksgiving; and having satisfied their thirst with joy in this torrent of delights, broke forth in canticles of praise for all Thy mercy towards sinners. Whilst these things happened I heard these words: "Consider how agreeable this concert of praise is, not only to My ears, but even to My most loving Heart; and beware for the future how you desire so importunately to be separated from the body, merely for the sake of being delivered from the flesh, in which I pour forth so freely the gifts of My grace; for the more unworthy they are to whom I condescend, the more I merit to be glorified for it by all creatures."

As thou didst give this consolation at the moment when I approached Thy life-giving Sacrament, as soon as I had recollected myself and formed my intention, as I was bound to do, Thou didst make known to me further in what manner, and with what intention, each one should approach to unite themselves to Thy sacred Body and Blood; so that, even if this Sacrament served for our condemnation, were it possible, the love of Thy love and of Thy glory would cause us to think nothing of this, provided that thereby Thy mercy shone forth still more in not refusing to give Thyself to those who are so utterly unworthy. Then I inquired concerning those who, from a consciousness of their unworthiness, abstain from Communion, fearing to profane by a presumptuous irreverence the sanctity of this Sacrament; and I received this blessed answer from Thee: "He who communicates from a pure desire of My glory, as I have said, can never communicate with irreverence." For which may eternal praise and glory be given to Thee for endless ages!

Chapter XXII *How St. Gertrude was admitted to the vision of God of the kiss of peace, and other similar favors.* I should be unjust, in recalling the gratuitous gifts which I have received from Thy charitable clemency, if I ungratefully passed over what was granted to my unworthiness, by Thy most loving clemency, during a certain Lent. For on the second Sunday, as they sang at Mass before the procession, the response which commences Vidi Dominum facie ad faciem, a marvelous and inestimable coruscation illuminated my soul with the light of Divine revelation, and it appeared to me that my face was pressed to another face, as St. Bernard says: "Not a form, but forming; not attracting the bodily eye, but rejoicing the heart; giving freely gifts of love, not merely in appearance but in reality."

In this most enchanting vision, Thine eyes, bright as the solar rays, appeared opposite to mine, and Thou alone knowest how Thou, my dearest Lord, affected not only my soul, but even my body and all my strength. Grant, therefore, that as long as I live I may prove myself Thy humble and devoted servant.

But even as the rose is more beautiful and gives forth a sweeter fragrance in the spring, when it flourishes, than in the winter, when it is dried up, and, like the remembrance of a joy that is past, rekindles in us some pleasure to think of it, so I desire, by some comparison, to declare what I felt in this most joyful vision, to extol Thy love, so that if those who read this receive similar or even greater favors, they may thereby be excited to acts of thanksgiving; and I myself, by recalling them frequently, will inflame the negligence of my gratitude beneath the rays of this burning glass. When Thou didst display Thy most adorable Face, the source of all blessedness, as I have said, embracing me, unworthy, a light of inestimable sweetness passed through Thy Deified eyes into mine, passing through my inmost being, operating in all my members with admirable power and sweetness: first, it appeared as if the marrow were taken from my bones; then, my flesh and bones appeared annihilated; so much so, that it seemed as if my substance no longer had any consciousness save of that Divine splendor, which shone in so inexplicable and delightful a manner that it was the source of the most inestimable pleasure and joy to my soul.

Oh, what shall I say further of this most sweet vision, if I may so term it? For all the eloquence in the world, if employed daily to persuade me, could never convince me that I should behold Thee more clearly even in glory, O my God, the only salvation of my soul, if Thou hadst not taught me by experience. I will dare to say that if anything, human or Divine, can exceed the blessedness of Thy embrace in this vision, as I consider, I may truly say that, unless thy Divine virtue possessed that person, the soul would never remain in the body after a momentary taste of this blessedness.

I render thanks to Thee, through the union of mutual love which reigns in the adorable Trinity, for what I have so often experienced, and that Thou hast deigned to favor me with Thy caresses; so that while I sat meditating, or reading the Canonical Hours, or saying the Office of the Dead, Thou hast often, during a single Psalm, embraced my soul many times with a kiss, which far surpasses the most fragrant perfumes or the sweetest honey; and I have often observed Thou didst look on me favorably in the condescending caresses Thou didst give to my soul. But though all these things were filled with an extreme sweetness, I declare, nevertheless, that nothing touched me so much as this majestic look of which I have spoken. For this, and for all the other favors, whose value Thou alone knowest, mayest Thou rejoice for ever in that ineffable sweetness surpassing all comprehension, which the Divine Persons communicate mutually to each other in the bosom of the Divinity!

May a like thanksgiving or, if possible, one even greater be rendered to Thee, for an extraordinary favor Thou hast granted me, of which Thou alone knowest, and which is so great, that I can neither fully express it by my feeble words, nor altogether pass it over in silence; and, lest I should lose the remembrance of it through my frailty, I write this to recall it to my memory and to excite my gratitude. But, my God, do not allow the meanest of Thy servants to be guilty of such an excess of madness as voluntarily to forget, even for a single instant, the gratitude which she is bound to have for the visits with which Thou hast honored her of Thy pure and gratuitous liberality, and which she has received for so many years without meriting them. For, although I am the most unworthy of all creatures, I declare, nevertheless, that these visits with which Thou hast favored me far surpass anything that could be merited during this life. I, therefore, implore Thy sweetest mercy to preserve this gift to me for Thy glory, with the same goodness with which Thou hast so liberally bestowed it, without any merit on my part, so that all creatures may glorify Thee eternally for it; since the more my unworthiness is made known, the more resplendently Thy mercy will shine forth.

Birgitta of Sweden
(1303–1373)

Birgitta, or Bridget, of Sweden, founder of the Brigittine Order, was a visionary woman of the fourteenth century who began recording her mystical experiences after her husband had passed away. The Brigittine Rule was revealed to her around 1346, in which Christ spoke to her personally. In 1349, Birgitta traveled to Rome, leaving her native country never to return. Like Catherine of Siena, Birgitta was politically active and her prophecies were politically charged; she wrote letters containing political and religious admonitions to the leaders of Europe. Her pilgrimages to Rome were imitated by Margery Kempe, who admired and fashioned her own prophetic identity after Birgitta's. The selections below, in which Birgitta, fashioned as the bride of Christ, both receives instruction regarding prophetic vocation and metes out instruction to Pope Gregory XI, demonstrate her style of political visionary writing. Some explanatory notes from the source text are included.

Book IV, Chapter 21. *Birgitta is Enouraged to Keep Teaching and Converting Others (c. 1350s, Italy).* The bride's words to God concerning his virtue and splendor, and the Virgin's consoling answer to the daughter, and about how God's good servants should not stop preaching and admonishing people, whether the people convert or not; the Virgin shows this by means of a comparison. "Blessed are you, my God, who are three and one: three persons in one nature. You are goodness and wisdom itself; you are beauty and power itself; you are justice and truth itself. All things live and subsist through you. You are like a flower that grows alone in a field. All those who draw near to it receive sweetness for their palate, an uplift for their spirits, a delight for their eyes and strength in every other limb. Likewise, all who come near to you become more beautiful by leaving sin behind, more wise by following your will rather than the flesh, more righteous by seeking the advantage of the soul and the glory of God. Therefore, most kind God, grant me to love that which pleases you, to resist temptations bravely, to scorn all worldly things and to keep you constantly in my memory."

The Mother answers: "This salutation came to you through the merits of good Jerome,[1] who left false wisdom and found true wisdom, who scorned earthly honor and was rewarded with God himself. Happy is such a Jerome, happy those who imitate his life and doctrine. He was a lover of widows, a mirror for those advancing toward perfection, a teacher of all truth and purity. But tell me, my daughter, what is troubling you in your heart?" She said: "A thought occurred to me that said, 'If you are good, your goodness is enough for you. Why judge and admonish and teach your betters, something that belongs neither to your state nor position?' This thought so hardens the spirit that it even neglects its own progress[2] and grows completely cold to God's love."

The Mother answers: "This thought has also held back many advanced souls from God. The devil hinders good people from speaking to the wicked so that they may not be

---

[1] "Jerome": church father, d. 420; creator of the standard translation of the Bible, the Vulgate, "False wisdom" refers to his rejection of classical learning following a vision in which he was told that he followed Cicero rather than Christ. His love "of widows" refers to his following among Roman noblewomen, including one named Paula [see Paula in this volume] and her daughter Eustochium. . . .

[2] "Neglects its own progress" renders "suiipsius obliuiscitur," literally, "forgets itself."

brought to feel compunction. He also hinders them from speaking to the good so that they will not be raised to a higher rank, for, when good people hear good doctrine, they are raised to a greater reward and a higher rank. For example, the eunuch[3] who was reading Isaiah would have received one of the lesser punishments in hell, but Philip met him and taught him a shortcut to heaven and so raised him up to a level of happiness. Likewise, Peter was sent to Cornelius.[4] If Cornelius had died beforehand, he would indeed have come to a place of rest because of his faith, but then came Peter and led him to the gateway to life. Similarly, Paul came to Denis[5] and led him to the reward of blessedness. For this reason, the friends of God should not grow tired in God's service but should labor on in order that the wicked may be made better and the good may attain a greater perfection.

"Anyone with the will to whisper in the ears of every passerby that Jesus Christ truly is the Son of God, and who struggles as far as he or she can for the conversion of others, even though no one or only a few convert, will still obtain the same reward as if all of them had converted. I will show you this by means of a comparison. If, on the order of their lord, two mercenaries dig through the hard rock of a mountain, and one of them were to find choice gold there, but the other none, both of them would be deserving of the same wages because of their work and their intention. In the same way, Paul, who converted many people and the other apostles, who converted fewer, were nevertheless all united in their intention. God's dispensation, however, remains hidden. One should therefore never give up, not even if only a few or none at all are open to God's words. As the thorn protects the rose and the donkey carries his master, so too the devil, like a thorn of sin, is as useful to the elect through the tribulations he causes as thorns

---

[3] "Eunuch"; cf. Acts 8:26–39.
[4] "Cornelius"; cf. Acts 10:1–33.
[5] "Denis," i.e., Denis (Dionysius) the Areopagite; cf. Acts 17:34.

are to roses. In this way, they are not stupidly overcome by the presumption of their hearts. Thus, just like a donkey, he conveys them to God's consolation and a greater reward."

Book IV, Chapter 143. *Birgitta's Reply to Pope Gregory XI's Request for a Sign (February 1373, Italy).* The fourth revelation sent by Blessed Birgitta to the pope in the month of July in the year of our Lord 1373. She wrote this to a certain hermit[6] who had once been bishop and who was then with the pope in Avignon.

Our Lord Jesus Christ told me, Reverend Bishop, to write you the following words for you to show to the pope.

"The Pope seeks a sign. Tell him that the Pharisees sought a sign and that I answered them that just as Jonah was in the belly of the whale for three days and nights,[7] so I, the Virgin's Son, was dead in the earth for three days and nights. After the promised sign, I, God's Son, suffered, died, and was buried and rose again and ascended into my glory. Thus, Pope Gregory has received the sign of my exhortation to save souls. Let him do with deeds what belongs to my honor. Let him struggle to save souls and return my church to its pristine state and to a better condition. Then he will experience the sign and rewards of eternal consolation. He will also have a second sign. If he does not obey my words and come to Italy, he will lose not only temporal goods but also spiritual ones, and he will feel troubled at heart so long as he lives. Though his heart may sometimes seem to have some relief, the remorse of his conscience and his inner troubles will stay with him. The third sign is that I, God, speak miraculously to a woman.[8] What is the purpose of this? What is the benefit of it, if not the salvation and good

---

[6] "A certain hermit," i.e., Alfonso of Jaén.
[7] "Pharisees . . . three days and nights"; cf. Matthew 12:38–41.
[8] "Speak miraculously to a woman": probably an allusion to Master Mathias's prologue . . .

of souls and the reformation of the wicked and the improvement of the good?

"Concerning the dispute between the pope and Barnabò,[9] I answer that it is loathsome to me beyond measure, for numberless souls are in peril because of it. It is therefore my will that they should reach an agreement. Even if the pope were to be expelled from his papacy, it would be better for him to humble himself and come to an agreement, should the occasion present itself, than to allow so many souls to perish in eternal damnation. Concerning the betterment of the kingdom of France, it will not be made known until the pope himself arrives in Italy.

"It is as though there were a gibbet from which hung a rope that a numberless crowd was pulling to one side while only one man was pulling it to the other. So it obviously is with the damnation of souls. A great many are working on it. This pope should gaze on me alone, though everyone else is dissuading him from coming to Rome and resisting it as much as they can. He should trust in me alone, and I will help him, and none of them will prevail over him. As chicks in a nest raise themselves up and clamor and rejoice when their mother comes, so I shall joyfully run out to meet him and raise him up and honor him in both soul and body."

The Lord spoke again: "Because the pope is in doubt as to whether he should come to Rome for sake of the reestablishment of the peace and of my church, I will that he should come next autumn. Let him know that he can do nothing more pleasing to me than to come to Italy."

---

[9] "Barnabò," i.e., Barnabò Visconti (1319–85), ruler of Milan, a soldier and statesman and opponent of the papacy.

Catherine of Siena
(1347–1380)

Catherine of Siena became a Dominican tertiary when she was 21 years old. Like Angela of Foligno, she joined a Third Order (laity who were active in a religious order) rather than becoming a nun. Members of a Third Order were not enclosed and could thus focus on performing good works in a broader community. Catherine was active in assisting the poor and the sick (this was plague time in Europe). Raymond of Capua, to whom the letter below is addressed, became her confessor in the mid-1370s, and together they entered the political fray leading up to and surrounding the schism within the church.

Catherine wrote letters as well as her more famous *Dialogue*, a text which was influential for later women writers, including Julian of Norwich. The letter below describes Catherine's divinely inspired political action and her irrepressible spirit in confronting the political injustices she witnessed.

To Brother Raimondo of Capua of the Order of the Preachers

In the Name of Jesus Christ crucified and of sweet Mary:

Dearest father in Christ sweet Jesus: I Catherine, servant and slave of the servants of Jesus Christ, write to you in His precious Blood: with desire to see you a faithful servant and bridegroom of truth, and of sweet Mary, that we may never look back for any reason in the world, nor for any tribulations which God might send you: but with firm hope, with the light of most holy faith, pass through this stormy sea in all truthfulness; and let us rejoice in endurance, not seeking our own glory, but the glory of God and the salvation of souls, as the glorious martyrs did, who for the sake of truth made them ready for death and for all torments, so that with their blood, shed for love of the Blood, they built the walls of Holy Church. Ah, sweet Blood, that dost raise the dead! Thou givest life, thou dost dissolve the shadows that darken the minds of reasonable creatures, and dost give us light! Sweet Blood, thou dost unite those who strive, thou dost clothe the naked, thou dost feed the hungry and give to drink to those [*sic*] who thirst for thee, and with the milk of thy sweetness thou dost nourish the little ones who have made themselves small by true humility, and innocent by true purity. Oh, holy Blood, who shall receive thee amiss? The lovers of themselves, because they do not perceive thy fragrance.

So, dearest and sweetest father, let us divest us and clothe us in truth, so we shall be faithful lovers. I tell you that today I will to begin again, in order that my sins may not hold me back from such a good as it is to give one's life for Christ crucified. For I see that in the past, through my faults, this has been denied me. I had desired very much, with a new intensity, increased in me beyond all custom, to endure without fault for the honor of God and the salvation of souls and the reformation and good of Holy Church, so that my heart was melting from the love and desire I had to lay down my life. This desire was blessed and grievous; blessed it was for the union that I felt with truth, and grievous it was for the oppression which I felt from the wrong against God, and the multitude of demons who overshadowed all the city, dimming the eye of the mind in human beings. Almost it seemed that God was letting them have their way, through justice and divine discipline. Therefore my life could not but dissolve in weeping, fearful for the great evil which seemed on the point of coming, and because peace was hindered for this reason. But in this great evil, God, who despises not the desire of His servants, and that sweet mother Mary, whose name was invoked with pained and dolorous and loving desires, granted that in all the tumult and the great upheaval that occurred, we may almost say that there were no human deaths, except those which justice inflicted. So the desire I had that God would show His providence and destroy the power of the demons that they might not do so much harm as they were ready to do, was fulfilled; but my desire to give my life for the Truth and the sweet Bride of Christ was not fulfilled. But the Eternal Bridegroom played a great joke on me, as Christopher will tell you more fully by word of mouth. So I have reason to weep, because the multitude of my iniquities was so great that I did not deserve that my blood should give life, or illumine darkened minds, or reconcile the sons with the father, or cement a stone in the mystical body of Holy Church. Nay, it seemed that the hands of him who wanted to kill me were bound. My words, "I am she. Take me, and let this family be," were a sword that pierced straight through his heart. O Babbo mine, feel a wonderful joy in yourself, for I never experienced in myself such mysteries, with so great joy! There was the sweetness of truth in it, the gladness of a clean and pure conscience; there was the fragrance of the sweet providence of God; there was the savor of the times of new martyrs, foretold as you know by the Eternal Truth. Tongue would not suffice to tell how great the good is that my soul feels. I seem to be so bound to my Creator that if I gave my body to be burned I could not satisfy the great mercy which I and my cherished sons and daughters have received.

All this I tell you that you may not conceive bitterness; but may feel an unspeakable delight, with softest gladness; and that you and I may begin to sorrow over my imperfection, because so great a good was hindered by my sin. How blessed my soul would have been had I given my blood for the sweet Bride, and for love of the Blood and the salvation of souls! Now let us rejoice and be faithful lovers.

I will not say more on this subject; I let Christopher tell this and other things. Only I want to say this: do you pray Christ on earth not to delay the peace because of what has happened, but make it all the more promptly, so that then the other great deeds may be wrought which he has to do for the honor of God and the reformation of Holy Church. For the condition of things has not been changed by this—nay, for the present the city is pacified suitably enough. Pray him to act swiftly; and I ask him this in mercy, for infinite wrongs against God which happen through the situation will thus be put an end to. Tell him to have pity and compassion on these souls which are in great darkness: and tell him to release me from prison swiftly; for unless peace is made it does not seem as if I could get out; and I would wish then to come where you are, to taste the blood of the martyrs, and to visit his Holiness, and to find myself with you once more, telling of the admirable mysteries which God has wrought at this time; with gladness of mind, and joyousness of heart, and increase of hope, in the light of most holy faith. I say no more to you. Remain in the holy and sweet grace of God. Sweet Jesus, Jesus Love.

Julian of Norwich
(1342–c. 1416)

At the age of 30, Dame Julian, as Margery Kempe calls her, had a visionary experience in the midst of serious illness. Her reflections on this experience and additional theological ruminations constitute the substance of her *Shewings*. After becoming an anchoress (a woman who committed to a pious life of seclusion, usually in a cell adjacent to a church), Julian (who may have been a nun, but was not necessarily) dictated or recorded her revelations. As Shakespeare's Hamlet would later exclaim, "O God, I could be bounded in a nutshell and count / myself a king of infinite space . . ." (2.2.248–9), so Julian, in one of the selections below, was shown a mystery of "all that is made" being contained within the space of a hazelnut. Among other remarkable features of Julian's work, her profoundly optimistic concept of God and her notion of a "homely," or familiar, loving relationship between herself and the deity that proclaims, "all shall be well, and all manner of things shall be well," have made her work widely read and admired.

Though Julian is easier to understand than Margery, glosses from the source text are provided as notes.

V. *How God is to us everything that is gode, tenderly wrap-pand us; and all thing that is made, in regard to Almighty it is nothing; and how man hath no rest till he nowteth himselfe and all thing for the love of God. The fifth chapter.*

In this same time our Lord shewed to me a ghostly sight of His homely[1] loveing. I saw that He is to us everything that is good and comfortable for us. He is oure clotheing, that for love wrappeth us, halsyth us, and all becloseth us[2] for tender love, that He may never leeve us, being to us althing that is gode as to myne understondyng. Also in this He shewed a littil thing the quantitye of an hesil nutt[3] in the palme of my hand, and it was as round as a balle. I lokid there upon with eye of my understondyng and thowte, What may this be? And it was generally answered thus: *It is all that is made.* I mervellid how it might lesten,[4] for methowte it might suddenly have fallen to nowte for littil. And I was answered in my understondyng, *It lesteth and ever shall, for God loveth it; and so all thing hath the being[5] be the love of God.*

In this littil thing I saw three properties: the first is that God made it, the second is that God loveth it, the third, that God kepith it. But what is to me sothly the maker, the keper, and the lover I canot tell, for till I am substantially onyd[6] to Him I may never have full rest ne very[7] blisse; that is to sey, that I be so festined to Him, that there is right nowte that is made betwix my God and me. It needyth us to have knoweing of the littlehede[8] of creatures and to nowtyn allthing that is made for to love and howe God that is unmade.[9] For this is the cause why we be not all in ease of herete and soule, for we sekyn[10] here rest in those things that is so littil, wherin is no

---

[1] **homely**, intimate.
[2] **wrappeth . . . becloseth us**, winds about us, embraces us, and entirely encloses us.
[3] **hesil nutt**, hazel nut.
[4] **lesten**, last.
[5] **the being**, existence.
[6] **substantially onyd**, integrally joined.
[7] **ne very**, nor true.
[8] **littlehede**, smallness.
[9] **howe**, have (see note); **unmade**, without creator.
[10] **herete**, heart; **sekyn**, seek.

rest, and know not our God that is almighty, al wise, all gode; for He is the very rest. God will be knowen, and Him liketh[11] that we rest in Him. For all that is beneth Him sufficeth not us. And this is the cause why that no soule is restid till it is nowted[12] of all things that is made. Whan[13] he is willfully now-tid for love, to have Him that is all, then is he abyl to receive ghostly rest.

Also our Lord God shewed that it is full gret plesance to Him that a sily[14] soule come to Him nakidly and pleynly and homely. For this is the kinde yernings[15] of the soule by the touching of the Holy Ghost, as be the understondyng that I have in this sheweing: "God of Thy goodnesse, give me Thyselfe, for Thou art enow[16] to me, and I may nothing aske that is less that may be full worshippe to Thee. And if I aske anything that is lesse, ever me wantith; but only in Thee I have all." And these words arn[17] full lovesome to the soule, and full nere, touchen the will of God and His goodness. For His goodness comprehendith all His creatures and all His blissid works and overpassith without end. For He is the endleshede, and He hath made us only to Himselfe and restorid us be His blissid passion, and kepith us in His blissid love; and all this is of His goodness.

XXVI. *The twelfth Revelation is that the Lord our God is al sovereyn beyng. Twenty-sixth chapter.*

And after this our Lorde shewid Hym more gloryfyed, as to my syte, than I saw Him beforne, wherin I was lernyd that our soule shal never have rest til it comith to Hym knowing that He is fulhede of joy, homley and curtesly blisful and very life.

---

[11] **Him liketh**, it pleases Him.
[12] **nowted**, stripped.
[13] **Whan**, When.
[14] **sily**, innocent, simple.
[15] **kinde yernings**, natural yearning.
[16] **enow**, enough.
[17] **arn**, are.

Our Lord Jesus oftentymes seyd, *I it am, I it am, I it am that is heyest, I it am that thou lovist, I it am that thou lykyst, I it am that thou servist, I it am that thou longyst, I it am that thou desyrist, I it am that thou menyst, I it am that is al, I it am that Holy Church prechyth and teachyth the, I am that shewed me here to thee.* The nombre of the words passyth my witte and al my understondyng and al my mights, and it arn the heyest, as to my syte. For therin is comprehendid, I cannot tellyn—but the joy that I saw in the shewyng of them passyth al that herte may willen and soule may desire; and therefore the words be not declaryd here. But every man, after the grace that God gevyth him in understondyng and lovyng receive hem in our Lord's menyng.

XXVII. *The thirteenth Revelation is that our Lord God wil that we have grete regard to all His deds that He hav don in the gret noblyth of al things makyng and of etc; how synne is not knowin but by the peyn. Twenty-seventh chapter.*

After this the Lord browte to my mynd the longyng that I had to Hym aforn. And I saw that nothyng letted[18] me but synne, and so I beheld generally in us al. And methowte, if synne had not a ben, we should al a ben clene and like to our Lord as He made us. And thus, in my foly, aforn this tyme, often I wondrid whi by the gret forseyng wysdam of God the begynyng of synne was not lettid.[19] For than, thowte me, al shuld a be wele. This steryng[20] was mikel to forsakyn, and nevertheless mornyng and sorow I made therefor without reason and discretion.

But Jesus, that in this vision enformid me of all that me nedyth, answerid by this word, and seyd: *Synne is behovabil,*[21] *but al shal be wel, and al shal be wel, and al manner of thyng*

---

[18] **letted**, hindered.
[19] **forseyng**, foreseeing; **lettid**, prevented.
[20] **a be**, have been; **steryng**, agitation.
[21] **behovabil**, necessary; fits in.

shal be wele. In this nakid word *synne,* our Lord browte to my
mynd generally al that is not good, and the shamfull dispite
and the utter nowtyng that He bare for us in this life, and His
dyeng, and al the peynys and passions of al His creatures,
gostly and bodyly—for we be all in party nowtid,[22] and we
shall be nowtid followyng our Master Jesus till we be full pur-
gyd, that is to sey, till we be fully nowtid of our dedly flesh and
of al our inward affections which arn not very good—and the
beholdyng of this with al peynys that ever wern[23] or ever shal
be; and with al these I understond the passion of Criste for
most peyne and overpassyng. And al this was shewid in a
touch, and redily passid over into comforte. For our good
Lord wold not that the soule were afferd[24] of this uggly syte.

But I saw not synne, for I beleve it hath no manner of substance ne no party of being, ne it myght not be knowin, but by
the peyne that it is cause of; and thus peyne—it is somethyng,
as to my syte, for a tyme, for it purgith and makyth us to
knowen our selfe and askyn mercy. For the passion of our
Lord is comforte to us agens al this, and so is His blissid wille.
And for the tender love that our good Lord hath to all that shal
be save, He comfortith redyly and swetely, menyng thus: *It is
sothe that synne is cause of all this peyne, but al shal be wele,
and al shall be wele, and all manner thing shal be wele.* These
words were seyd full tenderly, shewyng no manner of blame
to me ne to non that shall be safe. Than were it a gret unkind-
ness to blame or wonder on God for my synne, sythen[25] He
blamyth not me for synne. And in these same words I saw a
mervelous, hey privitye hid in God, which privity He shall
openly make knowen to us in Hevyn, in which knowyng we
shal verily see the cause why He suffrid synne to come, in
which syte we shall endlesly joyen in our Lord God.

---

[22] **in party nowtid**, partly despised.
[23] **wern**, were.
[24] **afferd**, afraid.
[25] **sythen**, since.

XXXII. *How al thyng shal be wele and Scripture fulfillid, and we must stedfastly holdyn us in the faith of Holy Chirch as is Crists wille. Thirty-second chapter.*

On[26] tyme our good Lord seid, *Al thyng shal be wele,* and another tyme He seid, *Thu shalt sen thiself that al manner thyng shal be wele.* And in these two, the soule toke sundry understondyng. On was this: that He wil we wetyn[27] that not only He takith hede to noble thyngs and to grete, but also to litil and to smale, to low and to simple, to on and to other. And so menyth He in that He seith, *Al manner thyngs shal be wele.* For He will we wetyn the leste thyng shal not be forgottyn. Another understondyng is this: that there be dedes evyl done in our syte and so grete harmes takyn, that it semyth to us that it were impossibil that ever it shuld cum to gode end, and upon this we loke sorowyng and morning[28] therefore, so that we cannot restyn us in the blisful beholdyng of God as we shuld doe. And the cause is this, that the use of our reason is now so blynd, so low, and so symple, that we cannot know that hey, mervelous wisdam, the myte, and the goodness, of the blisful Trinite; and thus menyth He wher He seith, *Thou shalt se thiself that al maner thyng shal be wele.* As if He seid, "Take now hede faithfuly and trostily,[29] and at the last end thou shalt verily sen it in fulhede of joye." And thus in these same five words afornseid, *I may make al thyngs wele* etc., I understond a myty comforte of al the works of our Lord God that arn for to comen.

Ther is a dede the which the blisful Trinite shal don in the last day, as to my syte. And whan the dede shall be and how it shal be done, it is onknown of all creatures that are beneath Criste, and shal be, till whan it is don. And the cause He wil we know is for He wil we be the more esyd in our soule and

---

[26] **On**, one.
[27] **On**, one; **wetyn**, understand.
[28] **loke**, look; **morning**, mourning.
[29] **trostily**, trustfully.

pesid[30] in love, levyng the beholdyng of al tempests that myte lettyn us of trewth, enjoyeng in Hym. This is the grete dede ordeynyd of our Lord God from without begynnyng, treasured and hid in His blissid breast, only knowen to Hymself, be which dede He shal make al thyngs wele. For like as the blisful Trinite made al thyngs of nowte, ryte so the same blissid Trinite shal make wele al that is not wele.

And in this syte I mervelid gretely and beheld our feith, merveland thus: Our feith is growndid in Goddys word, and it longyth to our feith that we levyn that Goddys word shal be savid in al things. And one peynt[31] of our feith is that many creatures shal be dampnyd—as Angells that fellyn out of Hevyn for pride which be now fends, and man in herth[32] that deyth oute of the feith of Holy Church, that is to say, thei that be ethen[33] men, and also man that hath receyvid Christendam and livith uncristen life, and so deyth out of charite—all these shall be dampnyd to Helle without end, as Holy Church techyth me to belevyn.

And stondyng[34] al this, methowte it was impossibil that al manner thyng should be wele as our Lord shewid in this tyme. And as to this I had no other answere in shewyng of our Lord God but this: *That[35] is impossible to the is not impossible to Me. I shal save My worde in al things, and I shal make al thing wele.* Thus I was tawte by the grace of God that I should stedfasty[36] hold me in the faith as I had afornehand understonden, and therewith that I should sadly levyn[37] that al thyng shal be wele, as our Lord shewid in the same tyme. For this is the great dede that our Lord shal done, in which dede He shal

---

[30] **pesid**, made peaceful.
[31] **peynt**, point.
[32] **herth**, earth.
[33] **ethen**, heathen.
[34] **And stondyng**, And this being so.
[35] **That**, What.
[36] **stedfasty**, steadfastly.
[37] **sadly levyn**, firmly believe.

save His word in al thing, and He shal make wele al that is not wele. And how it shal be don there is no creature benethe Criste that wot it, ne shal wetyn it, till it is don, as to the understondyng that I toke of our Lords menyng in this tyme.

Christine de Pisan
(1365–c. 1430)

These excerpts come from *The Book of the City of Ladies*, in which the narrator has spiritual dialogues with the divine ladies Reason, Rectitude, and Justice. Throughout the text, the highly educated Christine, whose father and husband served at the court of Charles V, defends women against typical misogynist views—Eve is redeemed, biblical and classical women described as exempla, and the city prepared for Mary, the lady of ladies. Christine confronts what we now might describe as the question of how to be a Christian and a feminist, and presents an apologia for women as Kassia had done before her and Aemilia Lanyer would do after.

II.30.1 *Christine speaks of the great benefit accrued and accruing every day to the world because of women.* [The narrator speaks] "My lady, I see the endless benefits which have accrued to the world through women and nevertheless these men claim that there is no evil which has not come into the world because of them."

"Fair friend," she [Rectitude] answered, "you can see from what I have already said to you that the contrary of what they say is true. For there is no man who could sum up the enormous benefits which have come about through women and which come about every day, and I proved this for you with the examples of the noble ladies who gave the sciences and arts to the world. But, if what I have said about the earthly benefits accruing thanks to women is not enough for you, I will tell you about the spiritual ones. Oh, how could any man be so heartless to forget that the door of Paradise was opened to him by a woman? As I told you before, it was opened by the Virgin Mary, and is there anything greater one could ask for than that God was made man? And who can forget the great benefits which mothers bring to their sons and which wives bring to their husbands? I implore them at the very least not to forget the advantages which touch upon spiritual good. Let us consider the Law of the Jews. If you recall the story of Moses, to whom God gave the written Law of the Jews, you will find that this holy prophet, through whom so much good has come about, was saved from death by a woman, just as I will tell you.

"In time when the Jews were in servitude to the kings of Egypt, it was foretold that a man would be born among the Hebrews who would lead the people of Israel out of servitude to the kings. When Moses, that noble leader, was born, his mother, not daring to nurse him, was forced to place him in a small basket and send him downstream. So it happened—according to the will of God who saves whatsoever pleases Him—that Thermutis, the daughter of Pharaoh, was playing on the riverbank at the very moment when the little basket floated by on the water, and she immediately had the basket brought to her in order to find out what was inside. When she saw that it was such a lovely child that a more beautiful child could not be imagined, she was terribly glad. She had him nursed and claimed him as her own, and, because through a miracle he would not take the breast of a woman of a foreign religion, she had him nursed by a Hebrew woman. When Moses, elected by God, was grown, it was he to whom our Lord gave the Law and who delivered the Jews from the hands of the Egyptians, and he passed through the Red Sea and was the leader and guide of the children of Israel. And this great benefit came to the Jews thanks to the woman who saved him."

III. *The first chapter tells how Justice led the Queen of Heaven to live in the City of Ladies.*

III.1.2 "'We greet you, Queen of Heaven, with the greeting which the Angel brought you, when he said, *Hail Mary*, which pleased you more than all other greetings. May all the devout sex of women humbly beseech you that it please you well to reside among them with grace and mercy, as their defender, protector, and guard against all assaults or enemies and of the world, that they may drink from the fountain of virtues which flows from you and be so satisfied that every sin and vice be abominable to them. Now come to us, Heavenly Queen, Temple of God, Cell and Cloister of the Holy Spirit, Vessel of the Trinity, Joy of the Angels, Star and Guide to those who have gone astray, Hope of True Believers. My Lady, what man is so brazen to dare think or say that the feminine sex is vile in beholding your dignity? For if all other women were bad, the light of your goodness so surpasses and transcends them that any remaining evil would vanish. Since God chose His spouse from among women, most excellent Lady, because of your honor, not only should men refrain from reproaching women but they should also hold them in great reverence.'"

The Virgin replied as follows: "O Justice, greatly beloved by my Son, I will live and abide most happily among my sisters and friends, for Reason, Rectitude, and you, as well as Nature, urge me to do so. They serve, praise, and honor me unceasingly, for I am and will always be the head of the feminine sex. This arrangement was present in the mind of God the Father from the start, revealed and ordained previously in the council of the Trinity."

Here Justice answered, while all the women knelt with their heads bowed, "My Lady, may honor and praise be given to your forever. Save us, our Lady, and pray for us to your Son who refuses you nothing."

III.2.1 *Concerning the sisters of Our Lady and Mary Magdalene.* "Now the incomparable Empress resides with us, regardless of whether it pleases the malicious slanderers. Her blessed sisters and Mary Magdalene must also dwell with her, for they stayed steadfastly with her, next to the Cross, during the entire Passion of her Son. What strong faith and deep love those women possess who did not forsake the Son of God who had been abandoned and deserted by all His Apostles. God has never reproached the love of women as weakness, as some men contend, for He placed the spark of fervent love in the hearts of the blessed Magdalene and of other ladies, indeed His approval of this love is clearly to be seen."

Margery Kempe
(c. 1373–1438)

Margery Kempe's spiritual autobiography was likely recorded in the 1430s. She dictated first to a male scribe, then to a priest. The narrative regales readers with stories of her ecstatic spiritual experiences, her struggle to remain celibate (despite the fact that she was married and had many children), her conversations and conflicts with the religious patriarchy of rural England and beyond, her pilgrimages to sacred sites and travels to Norway and Germany, and her dialogues with Jesus. Notably, Margery visited Julian of Norwich (see below) and imitated Birgitta of Sweden as she fashioned her prophetic identity. In the sections below, Kempe receives Christ's reassurance of his love and protection and an explanation for why she is so often moved to outbursts of weeping, which made her a strange, threatening spectacle in the communities she visited.

The text below may initially look daunting; however, a phonetic reading, sounding out the letters and syllables, renders the text in an English that *sounds* very much like ours, even if it doesn't look like it. In addition, the glosses in the source text are provided as notes below.

64. The creatur seyd unto hir Lord Crist Jhesu, "A, blisful Lord, I wolde I knew wherin I myth best love the and plesyn the and that my love wer as swet to the as me thynkyth that thy

love is unto me." Than owr swete Lord Jhesus, answeryng hys
creatur, seyd, "Dowtyr, yyf thu knew how swet thy love is unto
me, thu schuldist nevyr do other thyng but lovyn me wyth al
thyn hert. And therfor beleve wel, dowtyr, that my lofe is not
so swet to the as thy lofe is to me. Dowtyr, thu knowist not how
meche I lofe the, for it may not be knowyn in this werld how
meche it is, ne be felt as it is, for thu schuldist faylyn and
brestyn[1] and nevyr enduryn it for the joye that thu schuldist
fele.

"And therfor I mesur it as I wil to thi most ese and comfort.
But, dowtyr, thu schalt wel knowyn in an other worlde how
meche I lovyd the in erde, for ther thu schalt han gret cawse
to thankyn me. Ther thu schalt se wythowtyn ende every good
day that evyr I gaf the in erth of contemplacyon, of devocyon,
and of al the gret charité that I have govyn to the to the profyte
of thyn evyn cristen. For this schal be thy mete whan thu
comyst hom into hevyn. Ther is no clerk in al this world that
can, dowtyr, leryn[2] the bettyr than I can do, and, yyf thu wilt
be buxom[3] to my wyl, I schal be buxom to thy wil. Wher is a
bettyr charité than to wepyn for thi Lordys lofe? Thu wost wel,
dowtyr, that the devyl hath no charité, for he is ful wroth wyth
the and he myth owt hurtyn the, but he schal not deryn[4] the
saf a lityl in this world for to makyn the afeerd sumtyme, that
thu schuldist preyn[5] the myghtilier to me for grace and steryn
thy charité the mor to meward.[6] Ther is no clerk can spekyn
agens the lyfe whech I teche the, and, yyf he do, he is not
Goddys clerk; he is the develys clerk. I telle the ryth forsothe
that ther is no man in this world, yyf he wolde suffyr as meche

---

[1] **faylyn and brestyn**, fail and burst.
[2] **leryn**, learn, i.e., teach.
[3] **buxom**, obedient.
[4] **deryn**, harm.
[5] **preyn**, pray.
[6] **to meward**, toward me.

despite for my lofe wilfully as thu hast don and clevyn as sor[7]
unto me, not willyng for anythyng that may be do er seyd agen
hym forsakyn me, but I schal far ryth fayr wyth hym and be
ryth gracyowse unto hym, bothyn in this worlde and in the
other." Than seyd the creatur, "A, my derworthy Lord, this lyfe
schuldist thu schewyn to religiows men and to preistys." Owr
Lord seyd agen to hir, "Nay, nay, dowtyr, for that thyng that I
lofe best thei lofe not, and that is schamys, despitys, scornys,
and reprevys of the pepil, and therfor schal thei not have this
grace. For, dowtyr, I telle the, he that dredith the schamys of
the world may not parfytely lovyn God. And, dowtyr, undyr the
abyte of holynes is curyd[8] meche wykkydnes. Dowtyr, yyf thu
sey the wikkydnes that is wrowt in the werld as I do, thu schuldist have gret wondyr that I take not uttyr venjawns on hem.
But, dowtyr, I spar[9] for thy lofe. Thu wepist so every day for
mercy that I must nedys grawnt it the, and wil not the pepil
belevyn the goodnes that I werke in the for hem. Nevyrthelesse,
dowtyr, ther schal come a tyme whan thei schal be ryth fayn[10]
to belevyn the grace that I have govyn the for hem. And I schal
sey to hem whan thei arn passyd owt of this world, 'Lo, I
ordeynd hir to wepyn for hir synnes, and ye had hir in gret
despite, but hir charité wolde nevyr sesen for yow. And therfor, dowtyr, thei that arn good sowlys schal hyly thank me for
the grace and goodnes that I have gove the, and thei that arn
wikkyd schal grutchyn[11] and han gret peyn to suffyr the grace
that I schewe to the. And therfor I schal chastisyn hem as it
wer for myself." Sche preyd, "Nay, derworthy Lord Jhesu,
chastise no creatur for me. Thu wost wel, Lord, that I desyr no
venjawns, but I aske mercy and grace for alle men yyf it be thy
wille to grawnt it. Nevyrthelesse, Lord, rathyr than thei
schulde ben departyd fro the wythowtyn ende, chastise hem as

---

[7] **clevyn as sor**, cleave as closely.
[8] **abyte**, habit; **curyd**, covered.
[9] **spar**, spare (them).
[10] **fayn**, fain, eager.
[11] **grutchyn**, grudge, complain.

thu wilt thiselfe. It semyth, Lord, in my sowle that thu art ful
of charité, for thu seyst thu wilt not the deth of a synful man.
And thu seyst also thu wilt alle men ben savyd. Than, Lord, syn
thu woldist alle men schulde ben savyd, I must wyl the same,
and thu seyst thyself that I must lovyn myn evyn cristen[12] as
myn owyn self. And, Lord, thu knowist that I have wept and
sorwyd many yerys for I wolde be savyd, and so must I do for
myn evyn cristen.'

77. Whan the seyd creatur had first hyr wondirful cryis and
on a tyme was in gostly dalyawns wyth hir sovereyn Lord
Crist Jhesu, sche seyd, "Lord, why wilt thu gyf me swech crying that the pepil wondryth on me therfor and thei seyn that
I am in gret perel, for, as thei seyn, I am cawse that many
men synne on me. And thu knowist, Lord, that I wolde gevyn
no man cawse ne occasyon of synne yyf I myth, for I had
levar, Lord, ben in a preson of ten fadom[13] depe ther to cryin
and wepyn for my synne and for alle mennys synnys and spe-
cialy for thy lofe al my lyf tyme than I schulde gevyn the pepil
occasyon to synnyn on me wilfully.[14] Lord, the worlde may
not suffyr me to do thy wil ne to folwyn aftyr thi steryng, and
therfor I prey the, yyf it be thy wil, take thes cryingys fro me
in the tyme of sermownys that I cry not at thin holy prechyng
and late me havyn hem be myself alone so that I be not putt
fro heryng of thin holy prechyng and of thin holy wordys, for
grettar peyn may I not suffyr in this worlde than be put fro
thi holy worde heryng. And, yyf I wer in preson, my most
peyn schulde be the forberyng of thin holy wordys and of thin
holy sermownys. And, good Lord, yyf thu wilt algate[15] that I
crye, I prey the geve me it alone in my chambyr as meche as
evyr thu wilt and spar me amongys the pepil, yyf it plese the."

---

[12] **"evyn christen,"** i.e., fellow Christian (M.H.)
[13] **fadom**, fathoms.
[14] **to synnyn on me wilfully**, to sin willfully on account of me.
[15] **algate**, rather, prefer.

Owr merciful Lord Crist Jhesu answeryng to hir mende seyd,
"Dowtyr, prey not therfor; thu schalt not han thy desyr in this
thow my modyr and alle the seyntys in hevyn preye for the,
for I schal make the buxom to my wil that thu schalt criyn
whan I wil, and wher I wil, bothyn lowde and stille, for I teld
the, dowtyr, thu art myn and I am thyn, and so schalt thu be
wythowtyn ende. Dowtyr, thu seist how the planetys[16] ar
buxom to my wil, that sumtyme ther cum gret thundirkrakkys[17] and makyn the pepil ful sor afeerd. And sumtyme,
dowtyr, thu seest how I sende gret levenys[18] that brennyn
chirchys and howsys. Also sumtyme thu seest that I sende
gret wyndys that blowyn down stepelys,[19] howsys, and trees
owt of the erde and doth mech harm in many placys, and yet
may not the wynd be seyn but it may wel be felt. And ryth so,
dowtyr, I fare wyth the myth of my Godheed; it may not be
seyn wyth mannys eye, and yyt[20] it may wel be felt in a sympil
sowle wher likyth to werkyn grace, as I do in thi sowle. And,
as sodeynly as the levyn comith fro hevyn, so sodeynly come
I into thy sowle, and illumyn it wyth the lyght of grace and of
undirstandyng, and sett it al on fyr wyth lofe, and make the
fyr of lofe to brenne therin and purgyn it ful clene fro alle
erdly filth. And sumtyme, dowtyr, I make erdedenys[21] for to
feryn the pepil that thei schulde dredyn me. And so, dowtyr,
gostly have I don wyth the and wyth other chosyn sowlys that
schal ben savyd, for I turne the erthe of her hertys upsodown
and make hem sore afeerd that thei dredyn venjawnce
schulde fallyn on hem for her synnys. And so dedist thu, dowtyr, whan thu turnedist fyrst to me, and it is nedful that yong
begynnarys do so, but now, dowtyr, thu hast gret cawse to
lovyn me wel, for the parfyte charité that I gyf the puttyth

---

[16] **planetys**, planets.
[17] **thundirkrakkys**, thunder claps.
[18] **levenys**, lightning bolts.
[19] **stepelys**, steeples.
[20] **yyt**, yet.
[21] **erdedenys**, earthquakes.

away al drede fro the. And, thow other men settyn lityl be
the, I sett but the mor prys[22] be the. As sekyr as thu art of the
sunne whan thu seest it schynyn bryghtly, ryth so sekyr art
thu of the lofe of God at al tyme. Also, dowtyr, thu wost wel
that I send sumtyme many gret reynys and scharp schowerys,
and sumtyme but smale and softe dropis. And ryth so I far
wyth the, dowtyr, whan it likyth me to spekyn in thi sowle; I
gyf the sumtyme smale wepyngys and soft teerys for a tokyn
that I lofe the, and sumtyme I geve the gret cryis and ror-
yngys for to makyn the pepil aferd wyth the grace that I putte
in the into a tokyn that I wil that my modrys sorwe be knowyn
by the that men and women myth have the mor compassyon
of hir sorwe that sche suffyrd for me. And the thryd tokyn is
this, dowtyr, that what creatur wil takyn as mech sorwe for
my passyon as thu hast don many a tyme and wil sesyn of her
synnys that thei schal have the blys of hevyn wythowtyn ende.
The ferth tokyn is this: that any creatur in erthe, haf he be
nevyr so horrybyl a synner, he thar nevyr fallyn in dispeyr[23]
yyf he wyl takyn exampil of thy levyng and werkyn sumwhat
theraftyr as he may do. Also, dowtyr, the fifte tokyn is that I
wil thu knowe in thiself be the gret peyne that thu felist in
thyn hert whan thu cryist so sor for my lofe that it schal be
cawse thu schalt no peyn felyn whan thu art comyn owt of
this worlde and also that thu schalt have the lesse peyn in thy
deying, for thu hast so gret compassyon of my flesche I must
nede have compassyon of thi flesch. And therfor, dowtyr, suffyr the pepil to sey what thei wil of thi crying, for thu art
nothyng cawse of her synne. Dowtyr, the pepil synnyd on me,
and yet was I not cawse of her synne." Than sche seyd, "A,
Lord, blissyd mote thu be, for me thynkyth thu dost thiself al
that thu biddist me don. In Holy Writte, Lord, thu byddyst

---

[22] **prys**, price.
[23] **he thar nevyr fallyn in dispeyr**, he will never fall into despair because
of it (his past).

me lovyn myn enmys, and I wot wel that in al this werld was nevyr so gret an enmye to me as I have ben to the. Therfor, Lord, thei[24] I wer slayn an hundryd sithys[25] on a day, yyf it wer possibyl, for thy love, yet cowde I nevyr yeldyn the the goodnes that thu hast schewyd to me." Than answeryd owr Lord to hir and seyd, "I prey the, dowtyr, geve me not ellys but lofe. Thu maist nevyr plesyn me bettyr than havyn me evyr in thi lofe, ne thu schalt nevyr in no penawns that thu mayst do in erth plesyn me so meche as for to lovyn me. And, dowtyr, yyf thu wilt ben hey[26] in hevyn wyth me, kepe me alwey in thi mende as meche as thu mayst and forgete me not at thi mete, but thynk alwey that I sitte in thin hert and knowe every thowt that is therin, bothe good and ylle, and that I parceyve the lest[27] thynkyng and twynkelyng of thyn eye." Sche seyd agen to owr Lord, "Now trewly, Lord, I wolde I cowed lovyn the as mych as thu mythist makyn me to lovyn the. Yyf it wer possibyl, I wolde lovyn the as wel as alle the seyntys in hevyn lovyn the and as wel as alle the creaturys in erth myth lovyn the. And I wolde, Lord, for thi lofe be leyd nakyd on an hyrdil,[28] alle men to wonderyn on me for thi love, so it wer no perel to her sowlys, and thei to castyn slory[29] and slugge[30] on me, and be drawyn fro town to town every day my lyfetyme, yyf thu wer plesyd therby and no mannys sowle hyndryd, thi wil mote be fulfillyd and not myn."

---

[24] **thei**, though.
[25] **sithys**, times.
[26] **hey**, high.
[27] **lest**, least.
[28] **hyrdil**, hurdle.
[29] **so it wer no perel to her sowlys**, as long as it was no peril to their souls, i.e., as long as the sight did not imperil their souls; **slory**, slurry, thin mud.
[30] **slugge**, sludge, slime.

Teresa of Avila
(1515–1582)

St. Teresa of Avila was a Spanish Carmelite nun and mystic, and an important writer in the Spanish Renaissance. Her famous works *The Interior Castle* and *The Way of Perfection* emphasize the contemplative life, a life that Teresa describes and qualifies in the passage from her spiritual autobiography printed below. Teresa's experiences of spiritual ecstasy and union with the divine presence were somewhat alienating to the religious community around her, and more than one of her confessors suggested it was the devil working through her, not God. Teresa maintained that her experiences were at once corporeal and divine. In the passage below, Teresa discusses her feelings about contemplative prayer and meditating upon the corporeality of Christ, not forgetting that Christ was perfectly God and perfectly man. She gently admonishes her confessor and considers that perhaps other, purer souls than hers were equipped to meditate only upon the divinity; meanwhile, bound in the earthly vessel, she enjoins others to consider Christ's experience of corporeality.

Chapter XXII. *The saint shows how secure a way it is for those who give themselves to contemplation, not to raise their minds to high things unless our lord raise them himself, and how the humanity of Christ may serve as a means of reaching the highest degree of contemplation.*

I wish to make a remark here which, in my opinion, is very important; and if your Reverence consider it proper, it may serve as a word of advice to you; and, perhaps, you may even stand in need of it. I have read in some books which treat of prayer, that though the soul is not able of herself to arrive at this state, because everything is supernatural which our Lord works therein, yet that she may help herself towards this object, by raising her mind above all created things: and that so raising it with humility for many years, and having first passed through the "purgative" way, and then through the illuminative (I do not know why it is called by this name), the writers particularly advise persons to abstract themselves from all reflection on corporeal things, that so they may be able to arrive at the contemplation of the divinity. They say, that though it should be even the Humanity of Christ, yet it is some impediment for those who have advanced so far, and that it hinders persons from applying to the most perfect kind of contemplation. To support this opinion, they allege what our Lord said to His apostles, when He was ascending into heaven, respecting the descent of the Holy Ghost upon them. My opinion is, that if then they had that lively faith of our Lord being both God and man (as they had after the coming of the Holy Spirit), His corporal presence would have been no hindrance to them; for He spoke not thus to His mother, though she loved Him much more than all of them together. But they quote what our Lord said to His apostles, when He ascended into heaven, because it seems to them (as all the action is spiritual), that every corporeal object will prove a hindrance and obstacle to this kind of prayer; that they should consider themselves independent of creatures; that God surrounds them on all sides, and hence, that it should be their endeavor to see themselves engulfed in Him. To make use of this sometimes seems to me good: but to separate ourselves entirely from Christ, and to place His divine body in the same company with our miseries, or even with all created things, this I can by no means allow. May His Majesty grant that I may make myself understood. I do not wish to contradict these men, because they are spiritual and learned, and they know well what they say: it is also true, that God conducts souls through several ways and paths, as He did mine. And now I will declare some particulars thereof (in other matters I will not interfere); but I will only speak of the danger in which I found myself, because I acted conformably to what I read. I firmly believe, that whoever shall have arrived at the state of union, and not have passed further on, so as to have raptures and visions, and those other favors our Lord communicates to souls, may consider that which is mentioned above to be better, as I did. But if I had continued in that state, I believe I never should have arrived to where I am now, because, in my opinion, it is an error; though perhaps I myself may be deceived, but yet I will relate what happened to me.

When I had no director, and was engaged in reading those books alluded to above, I thought that by little and little I came to understand something; but I afterwards found out, that if our Lord had not been my teacher, I should have learnt very little by these books. It was a mere nothing which I understood, till His Majesty was pleased to make me know it by experience; neither did I know what I was doing. But when I began to understand a little about supernatural prayer (I mean the prayer of Quiet), I endeavored to avoid all corporeal objects, though I dared not exalt my soul; for knowing how very wicked I always was, I saw that this would be great presumption in me. But it seemed to me that I felt the presence of God, as indeed I did, and I endeavored to keep myself recollected with him. This is a sweet kind of prayer, if our Lord assist a soul therein, and the delight is very great; and when both the profit and the pleasure are perceived, no one could then make me return to the Humanity of Christ, because I thought that it was in reality an impediment to me. Lord of my soul! my Good! Jesus Christ crucified! I never call to mind the opinion which I then held, without feeling pain at the thought, for I think I committed a great treason against

Thee, though perhaps in ignorance. I have been especially devoted to the Passion of Christ throughout all my life, for this other circumstance happened in the latter part of it; I say, "in the latter part," before our Lord granted me the favor of having raptures and visions. I remained but a short time in this opinion, and then I always returned to regale myself with my Lord; and especially when I received the most blessed Sacrament, I always desired to have some picture or image of Him near my eyes, since I was not able to have Him as deeply engraven on my soul as I could wish. But is it possible, my Lord! a thought should ever have entered my mind, even for an hour, that Thou couldst be a hindrance to me in obtaining my greatest good? Whence have come all the blessings I have received, but from Thee? But I will not think I was in fault in this respect: rather I ought to pity myself for that which certainly proceeded from ignorance; and so Thou wert pleased in Thy goodness to remedy it, by giving me a person who delivered me from this error, and also by enabling me to see Thee so often, as I shall afterwards declare, that so I might the more clearly understand how great that ignorance of mine was; and likewise that I might declare the same to many persons, as I have already done, and declare it here also. I believe that the cause why many souls do not advance more, nor attain great liberty of soul when they arrive at the prayer of Union, is on this very account.

There are two reasons on which, it seems to me, this opinion may be grounded. And though what I am going to say may be of little or no importance, yet I will declare it, because I have found by experience, that my soul was not at all in a proper state till our Lord was pleased to give me light. For all those joys which she received came to me only by draughts; and when these were over, I did not find myself in such company, nor possessed of such strength to endure tribulations and temptations as I found afterwards. The first reason is, that there is a little want of humility, which, however, lies hidden in such a manner that it is not perceived by the person. And

who will be so proud and miserable as I was, even though he
should have passed his whole life in numerous acts of penance, in prayers, and all imaginable persecutions, as not even
then to consider himself very rich, and very well repaid, were
our Lord to allow him to stand at the foot of the cross with St.
John? No one but myself could help being content with such
a happiness as this, for I was a loser many ways in all those
things in which I ought to have been a gainer. But if our frail
nature, or our infirmities, will not allow us always to be meditating on the Passion (on account of its painfulness), what
should prevent us from remaining with Him now that He is
risen again to glory, since we have Him so near us in the
Blessed Sacrament? Nor need we behold Him there so
afflicted, torn in pieces, covered with blood, so weary going
along those rugged ways, so persecuted by those to whom He
did such good, and even not believed in by His own apostles:
because it is true that no one can bear always to be meditating
on all the sufferings which He endured. But in the Blessed
Sacrament we have Him without His enduring any pain, and
full of glory, giving strength to some and courage to others,
just as He did before He ascended into heaven. Here, in this
most adorable Sacrament, He is our companion, and it seems
as if it were not in His power to absent Himself one moment
from us: and yet I was able to remove myself from Thee,
under the pretext of serving Thee better! But when I was
offending Thee, I knew Thee not: and when I *did* know Thee,
how could I think of gaining by the way
I walked? Oh! what a rugged road I walked along! And now I
find I should have quite lost my way, if Thou hadst not con-
ducted me back to Thee; for as Thou wert near me, I saw I
had all good things. And whenever any affliction comes upon
me I consider how Thou wert treated before the Jews, and
then the affliction is very easily borne. With the presence of so
good a friend, and under the guidance of so valiant a captain,
who was in the foremost rank to suffer, everything can be
endured for His sake. He assists us and gives us strength, and

never fails in his promises: He is a true friend. I see clearly, that in order to please God, and to receive great favors from Him, He wishes to give them to us through the hands of this most sacred Humanity, in which His Majesty has said, He is "well pleased." Many, many times, I have known this truth by experience: besides, our Lord himself has told me so. I have also seen, that by this gate we must enter, if we wish His Sovereign Majesty to communicate great secrets to our souls.

Thus it is that I wish your Reverence not to choose any other way, though you should have arrived at the very height of contemplation; for here you will be safe, since this is our Lord, from whom all blessings come: if you consider His life, your own will be improved, for He is the very best pattern we can have. What can we desire more than to have so good a friend by our side, who will never desert us in our afflictions and tribulations, like men in the world do? Blessed is that man who loves our Lord truly, and who always has Him near to him. Let us consider the glorious St. Paul, who had the name of Jesus continually on his lips, because he had it deeply engraven in his heart. And from the time I have known this truth, I have carefully considered the life of many other great contemplative saints, and I have noticed that they walked along no other way. St. Francis shows this clearly by his wounds ("stigmata"); and St. Antony of Padua by the infant. St. Bernard took great delight in the humanity of our Lord; so also did St. Catherine of Siena, and many other saints, with whom your Reverence is better acquainted than I am. This abstraction from corporeal objects must be good, since persons of such spirituality tell us so; but, in my opinion, what they say must be understood of souls very far advanced in perfection; for till then it is evident that the Creator must be sought for by means of creatures. But I will not say much on this point, since all depends on the favors our Lord is pleased to show to any soul. What I wish to be understood is, that the most sacred Humanity of Christ must not be taken into this account; and let this point be well understood, that I would wish to know how to express myself properly.

When God is pleased to suspend all the powers of the soul, as He does in those kinds of prayer already mentioned, we have seen plainly that this presence is taken away from us, whether we will or no. But let it go; for what a happy loss is that whereby we gain more than what we thought we had lost! Then the whole soul is employed in loving Him whom the understanding has already endeavored to know; and she loves that which she did not comprehend, and enjoys what she could not have enjoyed, except only by losing her self for her greater gain, as I have already mentioned. But that we should accustom ourselves, by a kind of artifice, not to endeavor with all our strength to place always before our eyes—(and would it were always)—this most sacred Humanity: this, I repeat, is what I do not like, for it is as if the soul walked in the air, as the saying is, because she seems to have no support, however much she may fancy herself to be full of God.

Since we are mortal, it is very important for us as long as we live to represent our Lord's Humanity to our mind; for this is that other subject on which I wish to speak. The first (I said) proceeded from a want of a little humility, by presuming to raise the soul up before our Lord raised her; and not contenting herself with meditating on a subject so precious and sacred, she wishes to be Mary before she has labored with Martha. If our Lord should wish her to be Mary, we have nothing to fear then, though it should happen on the very first day of our entering His service. But let us consider the subject well, as I think I have mentioned before. This mote of little humility, though it may appear to be a mere nothing, will hinder us a great deal from advancing in contemplation.

Let us return now to the second point. Though we are not angels, but have bodies, yet to desire to make ourselves angels, while we are still upon the earth, is a kind of madness. But our thoughts require some support, generally speaking, though sometimes the soul may be so raised above herself, and often so full of God, as not to stand in need of any created object in order to recollect herself. But this is not so common when the soul is overpowered with business, or in persecutions and troubles, when she cannot have so much quiet: and in times also of dryness and dulness, Christ our Lord is found to be a very good friend, because we consider Him as man, and we behold Him full of weakness and afflictions, and there He keeps us company; and when once we acquire the custom, we shall find it very easy to keep Him close to us, though it will sometimes happen that we shall not be able to do either the one or the other. For this reason it will be well to do what I mentioned before, viz., not to strive to procure any consolation of soul, come what may; but willingly to embrace the cross of Christ, is very important. Our Lord was deprived of all consolation: He was left alone in his afflictions: let us not leave Him so. He will stretch out His hand to us, which will raise us up better than all our own endeavors; and yet He will absent Himself also whenever He shall think fit, and will raise the soul above herself when He wishes, as I have already mentioned.

God is much pleased to see a soul take, with humility, His Son for her intercessor; and He loves her so much, that even if His Majesty should desire to raise her up to a very high degree of contemplation, she acknowledges herself unworthy, and exclaims with St. Peter, "Depart from me, Lord! for I am a sinful man." This I have experienced myself, and in this manner has God guided my soul. Let others go (as I have said) by another shortcut; but what I have learnt is, that all this edifice of prayer is grounded on humility; and that the more the soul humbles herself in prayer, the more does God exalt her. I do not remember that He ever showed any of those singular favors (of which I shall speak hereafter) but only when I was in confusion at seeing myself so wicked: and His Majesty sometimes took care to make me understand certain things, which I never could have imagined myself, in order to help me to know myself better. I believe that when the soul does anything on her part to help herself on in this prayer of Union, yet the building will very quickly fall (though for the present her efforts may seem to advance her), because it has no solid foundation. And I am afraid she will never arrive at true poverty of spirit, which consists not in seeking comfort and pleasure in prayer (for the pleasures of this world are already forsaken), but consolation in afflictions, for the love of Him who always lived in them, and grace to remain patient under them, as well as quiet in aridities; arid though such souls cannot help feeling some pain thereat, yet they do not disturb themselves so much as some persons do, who imagine that if they are not always working with the understanding, and do not have sensible devotion, all is lost! As if they could merit so great a blessing by their own exertions! I do not mean to say, that they should not endeavor with care to keep themselves in the presence of God; but if they should be unable to have even one good thought (as I have mentioned in another place), yet they must not torment themselves. We are unprofitable servants, and what therefore can we fancy we are able to do? Our Lord is much better pleased that we should know this truth, and that we should consider ourselves only fit to be treated like some poor little asses, to turn the wheel for drawing the water spoken of before; for though these have their eyes blindfolded, and know not what they are doing, yet they draw up more water than the gardener can, with all his strength and exertions. We must walk in this way with liberty, and put ourselves in the hands of God. If His Majesty shall be pleased to rank us among the number of His confidential friends, we must accept the honor with a good will; but if not, we must be content to serve in inferior employments, and not sit down in the best place, as I have said elsewhere. God takes more care of us than we do ourselves, and knows what every one is fit for; what use then is it for him, who has already given his whole will to God, to govern himself? In my opinion, this is less to be allowed here than in the first degree of prayer, and it does us much more harm (if any error be committed), for these are supernatural blessings. If a man have a bad voice, however much he may force himself to sing, the voice will not thereby become good; but if God should please to give him a good voice, he need not torment himself. Let us, therefore, always beg of God to grant us His favors; and let the soul be resigned, though yet confiding in the greatness of God. And when she has received leave to remain at the feet of Christ, let her continue there in whatever way she can: let her imitate Mary Magdalen; and when she becomes strong, our Lord will take her into the desert.

Your Reverence will do well to keep yourself in this way, until you meet with some one else who has more experience than I have in this matter. If they be persons who are only beginning to delight in God, do not believe them, for they think they receive more profit and delight when they help themselves. Oh! how manifestly does God show His power, when He wills, without these poor helps! And so, whatever resistance we may make, He carries away the soul, just as some giant would carry away a straw. What an incredible thing would it be for a man to believe and to hope, that a toad could fly whenever it liked! Now I consider it to be a more difficult and absurd thing for our soul to raise herself up, without being raised by God, because it is laden with earth, and hindered by a thousand obstacles; and merely wishing to fly will be of little use to her. And though flying be more natural to a soul than to a toad, yet the soul is so deeply buried in mire, that she has lost the power of flying by her own fault.

I wish then to conclude with this remark, that whenever we meditate on Christ our Lord, we should ever remember the love wherewith He bestowed so many favors upon us, and how great that love was by His giving us such a pledge of it; for love produces love. And though we should be mere beginners, and withal very wicked, yet let us always be endeavoring to consider what I have been saying, and be exciting ourselves to love Him. If once our Lord shall be pleased to do us the favor of imprinting this love in our hearts, everything will become easy to us, and very quickly shall we begin to work, and this without any trouble. May His Majesty grant us this favor, since He knows how necessary it is for us; and we beg this favor by the great love He bore us, and for the sake of His divine son, who also loved us so much to His own cost. Amen.

One thing I would fain ask your Reverence, viz., how our Lord, when He begins to confer such high favors on a soul, as to raise her to a state of perfect contemplation (and this soul ought then most certainly to become perfect entirely and immediately, since a soul which receives such great favors should no longer desire the consolations of this world) how our Lord can in process of time abandon this soul, without maintaining her in the perfection of virtue, especially after she has received raptures and been accustomed to receive other favors; for the more she becomes disengaged from creatures, the more highly is she favored, considering, too, how when our Lord enters a soul He can sanctify her in a moment? This I desire to know, for I do not understand it, though I know well there is a difference between the strength which these raptures give in the beginning, when they continue only for the twinkling of an eye, and between the strength which the soul receives when they continue longer. But the doubt often occurs to me, whether the cause of this may not be, that the soul does not give herself up entirely to God, till His Majesty leads her little by little, and makes her determine at once, and gives her the strength of a full-grown man, that so she may trample everything under her feet, just as Mary Magdalen did so quickly. And so does He do to others, in proportion as they co-operate with Him, and as they allow His Majesty to dispose of them according to His own good pleasure; for we cannot but believe, that even in this life God rewards us a hundredfold.

I thought also of this comparison: that supposing what is given to beginners as well as to proficients be all the same, it is like a delicious viand whereof many persons eat; that they who eat little retain the sweet taste of it only for a short time, and they who eat more are enabled to subsist, but that they who feed plentifully on it receive life and strength. A soul may even feed so often and so fully on this food of life, as to have no relish at all for anything but that food, because she derives great benefit therefrom. Her taste also is so accustomed to this sweetness, that she would rather cease to exist than feed on other things, all of which would only serve to take away the good taste which the former food left on her lips. Besides, the conversation and company of a holy person does not do us so much good in one day as in many; but we may, by the Divine assistance, become like unto Him by remaining long with Him. Finally, the chief point depends upon God, to whom and when He is pleased to give His graces: but it is important to remember, that he who begins to receive this favor must resolve to disengage himself from everything, and to esteem the favors of our Lord as highly as they deserve.

It also seems to me as if His Majesty were resolved to try who they are that love Him whether this soul or that: and that He likewise wishes to discover who He is Himself, by giving us such excessive delights to quicken our faith, if it should be dead or weak, about those blessings He intends to give the soul: and He says: "Behold! this is but a drop of that immense ocean of blessing which I mean to give to those that love Me." And when He sees that we receive them as He gives them, He then gives us Himself. He loves those who love Him: and what a good friend, and who more worthy to be loved! O Lord of my soul! who will give me words that I might make men understand what Thou dost give to those who trust in Thee, and what they lose who arrive at this state and yet remain attached to themselves? Do not permit this, Lord! since Thou dost so much in coming to so wicked a place as my heart. Be Thou blessed forever and ever.

And now I wish to entreat your Reverence, that should you mention these matters on prayer, concerning which I have written, you would do so only to spiritual persons; because if they understand only one way, or have remained stationary half-way, they cannot judge correctly. There are some whom

God quickly raises to a very sublime degree, and they may think that others also might arrive there, and keep the understanding quiet, without making use of corporeal objects as means; such persons, however, will remain as dry as a stick. And some who have enjoyed a little the Prayer of Quiet, presently imagine, that as they have reached one degree they may reach the other; but these, instead of advancing, go backwards, as I have mentioned before. Thus, in all these matters both experience and prudence are necessary; and may our Lord in his goodness grant them to us.

Grace Mildmay
(1552–1620)

Lady Grace Mildmay was born into a landed aristocratic family and married into the wealthy Mildmay
family. Her father-in-law, Walther, and husband,
Anthony, both served at Elizabeth's court. Anthony
traveled a great deal and the couple had only one child,
a daughter. Anthony seems not to have been particularly enthusiastic about their marriage, which had been
arranged by their families (as was customary, especially
among the upper class). Later in their marriage, the
Mildmays dealt with litigation over family lands, a not
uncommon annoyance among the landed aristocracy
who would guard their inheritance, or sue for it,
fiercely.

Grace Mildmay is an extraordinary writer; her work
includes autobiography, spiritual reflections addressed
to her daughter, the Lady Fane, and medical guidance,
including recipes for treatments and tinctures. Her
spiritual meditations, selections from which are
included below, bear similarities to other women's
writings, such as Dhuoda's and Angela's, in this volume,
as they include the language of the Song of Songs as
well as reflections on theology and admonitions to right
conduct.

Occasion of Meditation. I was acquainted with a great
divine (in my youth), a learned preacher and truly mortified
from the world and he gave all that he had to the poor even to

the very clothes of his back, an unspotted and holy man in all his life and conversation. This man coming to the house where I was, at his departure from thence, as he was going out at the gate, he turned back towards me three several times, going from me and turning again to me, repeating these words following, shaking me hard by the hand and looking up to heaven in a most zealous manner. "Hold fast by Christ Jesus, hold fast by Christ Jesus, hold fast by Christ Jesus. He is the only man that liveth, all men are but dead and in Christ Jesus we shall all live."

Which words I take to import thus much: that I should say unto my soul, awake, awake, awake from sin, why sleepest thou therein? Arise, arise, arise unto righteousness and call upon thy God. Come away, come away, come away from all transitory shadows of this life unto the true substance, even unto Christ Jesus, to his heavenly kingdom, to his peace, to his joy and to everlasting life in him together with God his heavenly father and the holy ghost, three persons and one eternal God . . .

And as soon as we receive the benefits and blessings from God, let us give and distribute the same unto the needy, as nurses when their breasts be full are never quiet until they be drawn. Let us not spend and employ the gifts of God vainly, idly or unfruitfully upon our lusts and vain and needless delights, for the which we shall give an account (as for talents of goods lent) and for our time also which is but limited. Whilst we have time, let us do good unto all, in the name of the Lord, from whom all goodness proceedeth, and call upon him whilst he is near, in and for all things, whereby we may receive new supplies from God to furnish our store and maintain the work of our benevolence.

We are too careful and costly in our superfluous and unnecessary meats, drinks, and apparel and spend too much time therein, thinking all charges too little that are bestowed thereupon. And also we delight too much in play at cards and dice and in the pleasures of our flesh and going to plays and in many lewd and idle sports which draweth us from God and our goods from us, whereby mountains of treasures and revenues have been consumed and brought to nothing and we ourselves cast into poverty, left naked and become poor amongst the company of them which are constrained to beg, whose necessities we regarded not.

But if we did use our plenty well in those good uses for the which God hath given them unto us, we should be sure never to want but be indued with the love of God and receive from him blessing after blessing as we make the needy blessed and multiply the praises of God thereby. Spending our time and goods in this manner, we give thanks unto God for his benefits and publish his holy name and the magnificence thereof universally for his bountiful hand stretched out upon us from one hand to another, so that all our hands, hearts, and eyes may be lifted up together unto God and for one another.

Oh what a quiet mind shall that man possess which endeavoreth himself therein. It is neither to be expressed nor yet to be conceived. For when we shall cast off that heavy burthen which this world putteth upon every one that is born thereinto, all the trouble and crosses thereof will be more easy unto us and we shall pass them over with less danger to our own soul and conscience through the tender mercies of God, giving ourselves wholly unto God and to serve that one master only.

The Spouse of Christ. . . . My beloved is as a bundle of myrrh unto me, he shall lie between my breasts. My beloved is as a cluster of camphor unto me. His lips are like lilies, dropping down pure myrrh. His mouth is as sweet things and he is wholly delectable. His countenance is as Lebanon, excellent as the cedars (which signify and offer unto us all good things above the capacity of man to desire), until the day break and the shadows fly away. Return my welbeloved and be like a roe or a young hart, upon the mountains of Bether. Go from me but come again quickly and tarry not. In my bed let me seek my welbeloved. Yea, let me arise early to seek thee in all places, in all companies, in all opportunities and above all things, until I find thee and then let me take fast hold on thee and never leave thee.

Our Assurance in Christ, God's Love Toward Us. These things have I written unto you, that believe in the name of the son of God, that you may believe in the name of the son of God. And this is the assurance that we have in him if we ask any thing according to his will, he heareth us. And if we know that he heareth us, whatsoever we ask, we know that we have the petition that we have desired of him. God is love and he that dwelleth in love, dwelleth in God and God in him. In this appeared the love of God, because God sent his only begotten son into the world, that we might live through him. Herein is love, not that we loved God but that he loved us and sent his son to be a reconciliation for our sins. If God so loved us we ought also to love one another. If we love one another, God dwelleth in us and his love is perfect in us. Whosoever hath this world's good and seeth his brother have need and shutteth his compassion from him, how dwelleth the love of God in him? Let us not love in word, neither in tongue only but in deed and in truth. For thereby we know that we are of the truth and shall before him assure our hearts.

[Preparation for Death]. As long as I live, I will hope and live in hope . . . this anchor of our hope should not decay in us, nor fail us, the precious box of balm and sweet ointment was broken when Christ was crucified upon the cross and poured out upon us from all his blessed parts, that every one of us might receive the sweetness and fruitfulness thereof and be encouraged and strengthened in his holdfast, never to give over until the end.

It is time for me to prepare myself unto my end, for being old and almost aged I know my days hasten thereunto. First let me discharge and disburthen my mind of all superfluous and needless cares of this life, either for the times present or to come, all which are in the hands of God to dispose of at his will. All my dear children and friends in whom my chiefest worldly comforts doth consist, I bequeath them all unto God, knowing that he is able to keep all that is committed unto him. Beseeching him (from the bottom of my heart) to preserve and bless them and their godly generations for ever, if it be his holy will. And be their safe protection from Satan, the flesh and the world and defend them in all dangers which these perilous times of the latter age of the world shall bring forth. And let the same God replenish their minds from time to time, with a true understanding and judgment to discern rightly of earthly things, that they be not seduced by them and the vanities thereof, but let heaven be their object and continual apprehension, desires and expectation. What are the things of greatest moment, worthy to be remembered from my birth unto this day? Even that our sins have not been imputed unto us and that we are not confounded, which is through the only love of God the father, the mercy of Christ his son and the graces of the Holy Ghost. Let us cast all our care upon God, for he careth for us, in him we live, in him we move and have our being. We can do nothing but by him, nor have any thing but from him.

Mary Sidney Herbert, Countess of Pembroke (1561–1621)

Mary Sidney was the sister of writer Philip Sidney (whose works include the *Defense of Poesie* and *Astrophil and Stella*). She was highly educated, and her family was closely affiliated with the Elizabethan court. She married Henry Herbert, the Earl of Pembroke. As Countess of Pembroke, Mary became a patron of the arts, and thus was the dedicatee of poems from several highly regarded Elizabethan poets. Mary Sidney Herbert and Philip Sidney were very close, and what is known as the Sidney Psalter, begun by Philip, was completed by Mary after his death. The manuscript was circulated among and highly regarded by the family's aristocratic circle.

Psalm 52

TYRANT, why swell'st thou thus,
    Of mischief vaunting?
Since help from God to us
    Is never wanting.
Lewd lies thy tongue contrives,   5
    Loud lies it soundeth;
Sharper than sharpest knives
    With lies it woundeth.
Falsehood thy wit approves,
    All truth rejected: 10

Thy will all vices loves,
    Virtue neglected.
Not words from cursed thee,
    But gulfs are poured;
Gulfs wherein daily be   15
    Good men devoured.
Think'st thou to bear it so?
    God shall displace thee;
God shall thee overthrow,
    Crush thee, deface thee.   20
The just shall fearing see
    These fearful chances,
And laughing shoot at thee
    With scornful glances.
Lo, lo, the wretched wight,   25
    Who God disdaining,
His mischief made his might,
    His guard his gaining.
I as an olive tree
    Still green shall flourish: 30
God's house the soil shall be
    My roots to nourish.
My trust in his true love
    Truly attending,
Shall never thence remove,   35
    Never see ending.
Thee will I honor still,
    Lord, for this justice;
There fix my hopes I will
    Where thy saints' trust is.   40
Thy saints trust in thy name,
    Therein they joy them:
Protected by the same,
    Naught can annoy them.

(Wr. probably before 1599; pub. 1823)

Psalm 139

O LORD, O Lord, in me there lieth nought
    But to thy search revealed lies,
        For when I sit
        Thou markest it;
    No less thou notest when I rise;   5
Yea, closest closet of my thought
    Hath open windows to thine eyes.
Thou walkest with me when I walk;
    When to my bed for rest I go,
        I find thee there,   10
        And everywhere:
Not youngest thought in me doth grow,
No, not one word I cast to talk
    But yet unuttered thou dost know.
If forth I march, thou goest before,   15
    If back I turn, thou com'st behind:
        So forth nor back
        Thy guard I lack,
Nay on me too, thy hand I find.
Well I thy wisdom may adore,   20
    But never reach with earthy mind.
To shun thy notice, leave thine eye,
    O whither might I take my way?
        To starry sphere?
        Thy throne is there.   25
    To dead men's undelightsome stay?
There is thy walk, and there to lie
    Unknown, in vain I should assay.
O sun, whom light nor flight can match,
    Suppose thy lightful flightful wings   30
        Thou lend to me,
        And I could flee
    As far as thee the evening brings:
Even led to west he would me catch,

Nor should I lurk with western things.　35
Do thou thy best, O secret night,
In sable veil to cover me:
Thy sable veil
Shall vainly fail;
With day unmasked my night shall be,　40
For night is day, and darkness light,
O father of all lights, to thee.
Each inmost piece in me is thine:
While yet I in my mother dwelt,
All that me clad　45
From thee I had.
Thou in my frame hast strangely dealt:
Needs in my praise thy works must shine
So inly them my thoughts have felt.
Thou, how my back was beam-wise laid,　50
And raft'ring of my ribs, dost know;
Know'st every point
Of bone and joint,
How to this whole these parts did grow,
In brave embroid'ry fair arrayed,　55
Though wrought in shop both dark and low.
Nay fashionless, ere form I took,
Thy all and more beholding eye
My shapeless shape
Could not escape:　60
All these time framed successively
Ere one had being, in the book
Of thy foresight enrolled did lie.
My God, how I these studies prize,
That do thy hidden workings show!　65
Whose sum is such
No sum so much,
Nay, summed as sand they sumless grow.
I lie to sleep, from sleep I rise,
Yet still in thought with thee I go.　70

My God, if thou but one wouldst kill,
>   Then straight would leave my further chase
>>   This cursed brood
>>   Inured to blood,
>   Whose graceless taunts at thy disgrace   75
Have aimed oft; and hating still
>   Would with proud lies thy truth outface.
Hate not I them, who thee do hate?
>   Thine, Lord, I will the censure be.
>>   Detest I not   80
>>   The cankered knot
>   Whom I against thee banded see?
O Lord, thou know'st in highest rate
>   I hate them all as foes to me.
Search me, my God, and prove my heart,   85
>   Examine me, and try my thought;
>>   And mark in me
>>   If ought there be
>   That hath with cause their anger wrought.
If not (as not) my life's each part,   90
>   Lord, safely guide from danger brought.

(Wr. probably before 1599; pub. 1823.)

Aemilia Lanyer
(1569–1645)

Aemilia Lanyer's poetic work, *Salve Deus Rex Judaeorum*, was published in 1611, when she was in her forties. The book bears dedicatory addresses to a number of aristocratic and courtly women, including Queen Anne, Lucy, Countess of Bedford, Lady Arabella Stuart, Mary Sidney Herbert, and others. The text also includes the first English "country house" poem to be published, "The Description of Cookeham," an encomium in praise of the estate where Lanyer spent time as a young woman, with Margaret, Countess of Cumberland, and her daughter, Anne Clifford. This evidence suggests that although Lanyer herself was not from an aristocratic background, she moved in high circles.

Salve Deus Rex Judaeorum shares characteristics with the works of Kassia and Christine de Pisan, among others, especially in that it is an apologia for women and a revision of the misogynist myth that blames Eve for the sin in the world. The line numbers and marginalia are preserved from the source text.

Most blessed daughters of Jerusalem,   985
Who found such favor in your Saviors sight,
To turne his face when you did pitie him;
Your tearefull eyes, beheld his eies more
     bright;
Your Faith and Love unto such grace did clime,

To have reflection from this Heav'nly Light: 990
    Your Eagles eyes did gaze against this
        Sunne,
    Your hearts did thinke, he dead, the
        world were done.
When spightfull men with torments did
    oppresse
Th'afflicted body of this innocent Dove,
Poore women seeing how much they did
    transgresse,   995
By teares, by sighes, by cries intreat, nay
    prove,
What may be done among the thickest presse,
They labor still these tyrants hearts to move;
    In pitie and compassion to forbeare
    Their whipping, spurning, tearing of
        his haire.   1000
But all in vaine, their malice hath no end,
Their hearts more hard than flint, or marble
    stone;
Now to his griefe, his greatnesse they attend,
When he (God knowes) had rather be alone;
They are his guard, yet seeke all meanes
    to offend: 1005
Well may he grieve, well may he sigh and
    groane,
    Under the burthen of a heavy crosse,
    He faintly goes to make their gaine his
        losse.
His woefull Mother wayting on her Sonne,   The sorrow
All comfortlesse in depth of sorow drowned;   1010 of the
Her griefes extreame, although but new begun,   Virgin Marie.
To see his bleeding body oft shee swouned;
How could shee choose but thinke her selfe
    undone,

He dying, with whose glory shee was crowned?
    None ever lost so great a losse as shee,   1015
    Beeing Sonne, and Father of Eternitie.
Her teares did wash away his pretious blood,
That sinners might not tread it under feet
To worship him, and that it did her good
Upon her knees, although in open street,   1020
Knowing he was the Jessie floure and bud,
That must be gath'red when it smell'd most
      sweet:
    Her Sonne, her Husband, Father,
      Saviour, King,
    Whose death killd Death, and tooke
      away his sting.
Most blessed Virgin, in whose faultlesse fruit,   1025
All Nations of the earth must needes rejoyce,
No Creature having sence though ne'r so
    brute,
But joyes and trembles when they heare his
    voyce;
His wisedome strikes the wisest persons
    mute,
Faire chosen vessell, happy in his choyce: 1030
    Deere Mother of our Lord, whose
      reverend name,
    All people Blessed call, and spread
      thy fame.
For the Almightie magnified thee,
And looked downe upon thy meane estate;
Thy lowly mind, and unstain'd Chastitie,   1035
Did pleade for Love at great Jehovaes gate,
Who sending swift-wing'd Gabriel unto thee,
His holy will and pleasure to relate;
    To thee most beauteous Queene of
      Woman-kind,
    The Angell did unfold his Makers mind.   1040

He thus beganne, Haile Mary full of grace,

The Salutation
of the Virgin.

Thou freely art beloved of the Lord,
He is with thee, behold thy happy case;
    Marie.
What endlesse comfort did these words
    afford
To thee that saw'st an Angell in the place   1045
Proclaime thy Virtues worth, and to record
    Thee blessed among women: that thy
        praise
    Should last so many worlds beyond thy
        daies.
Loe, this high message to thy troubled spirit,
He doth deliver in the plainest sence;   1050
Sayes, Thou shouldst beare a Sonne that shal
    inherit
His Father Davids throne, free from offence,
Call's him that Holy thing, by whose pure merit
We must be sav'd, tels what he is, of whence;
    His worth, his greatnesse, what his
        name must be,   1055
    Who should be call'd the Sonne of the
        most High.
He cheeres thy troubled soule, bids thee
    not feare;
When thy pure thoughts could hardly
    apprehend
This salutation, when he did appeare;
Nor couldst thou judge, whereto those words
    did tend;   1060
His pure aspect did moove thy modest
    cheere
To muse, yet joy that God vouchsaf'd to send
    His glorious Angel; who did thee assure
        To beare a child, although a Virgin pure.
Nay more, thy Sonne should Rule and Raigne

       for ever;   1065
Yea, of his Kingdom there should be no end;
Over the house of Jacob, Heavens great Giver
Would give him powre, and to that end did
      send
His faithfull servant Gabriel to deliver
To thy chast eares no word that might offend: 1070
      But that this blessed Infant borne of
         thee,
        Thy Sonne, The onely Sonne of God
         should be.

When on the knees of thy submissive heart
Thou humbly didst demand, How that
      should be?
Thy virgin thoughts did thinke, none could
      impart   1075
This great good hap, and blessing unto thee;
Farre from desire of any man thou art,
Knowing not one, thou art from all men free:
      When he, to answere this thy chaste
         desire,
        Gives thee more cause to wonder
         and admire.   1080
That thou a blessed Virgin shoulst remaine,
Yea that the holy Ghost should come on thee
A maiden Mother, subject to no paine,
For highest powre should overshadow thee:
Could thy faire eyes from teares of joy
      refraine,   1085
When God look'd downe upon thy poore
      degree?
        Making thee Servant, Mother, Wife,
         and Nurse
        To Heavens bright King, that freed
         us from the curse.

Thus beeing crown'd with glory from above,
Grace and Perfection resting in thy breast,   1090
Thy humble answer doth approove thy Love,
And all these sayings in thy heart doe rest:
Thy Child a Lambe, and thou a Turtle dove,
Above all other women highly blest;
    To find such favor in his glorious sight,   1095
    In whom thy heart and soule doe
        most delight.

Lady Eleanor Davies
(1590–1652)

The Lady Eleanor Davies was a controversial figure who wrote prolifically prior to and during the civil wars in England. She was married to the poet John Davies in 1609, and lived in Ireland where her husband was attorney-general for several years. The couple had three children, but only their daughter Lucy (who would marry the earl of Huntingdon) survived.

Eleanor Davies had her first prophetic experience in 1625 and regularly prophesied and published her work after that. Her prophecies aroused anger in a number of people, including her husband, who passed away as she had predicted. She married Archibald Douglas in 1627, and continued to gain fame, or notoriety, for her prophecies. Her prediction that Charles I's favorite, the Duke of Buckingham, would die was not particularly well received, and she angered Archbishop Laud as well. Despite the consternation of Laud and others, Davies printed numerous pamphlets during her lifetime, even printing tracts overseas and having them imported into England in order to evade censorship. Davies was fond of anagrams and she frequently drew on biblical imagery, including that of the Books of Daniel and Revelation. The text below provides her testimony regarding her gift of prophecy and demonstrates Davies's style of prophesying about her contemporary context through the lens of Old Testament language and imagery.

The Lady Eleanor, her appeale to the high Court of Parliament.

Epigraph:

DAN.2.34. Thou sawest till that a Stone was cut out without hands, which smote the Image upon the feete: That of Iron, and Clay, and brake them in peeces, &c.

Here these touching the Iron-age, remaines of time, a tast thereof; the Sonnes of the Prophets for their use, needlesse; as into the water to cast a Logg, wherein a sticke cut downe, but thrown sufficeth, or to give a touch, &c. As farre either from building upon others foundation, theirs &c. The lanthorne unusefull, when the Moone giving light at full, not trespassing in that way here, nor borrowing either &c. And so farther of the latter dayes, these even being become drosse changed, even commanded these by him.

The Judge all-sufficient, God able to change all, and them reforme: As doubtlesse the end, the finall day before of doome refined reformed to bee: to this end commended by us, and being high time to make some preparation; the tydings of a troublesome time cut of, unfruitfull, &c.

In short shewed, those sharp dayes shortned, the brittle feete parted those, a warning peece, as followeth.

In peeces broken, destroyed at the last, though nothing than mettle lasting more: That stone then unmoveable invincible, the everlasting Law, as the workemanship of the Creators finger, moreover his heavie hand therewith: None other that great Image but spirituall aspiring *Babylon* the fall of both, the other Babell likewise that taken, going before the end of the World; like this dreame the World gone in a moment. And before the worlds departing, not without a Cuttng blow threatned forthwith, as when that hasty Decree sent forth his Proclamation for his owne Nation; those wise men to be destroyed. That first borne Monarchy, Babylons great revolution, visible even in our Horizon, that end or time, closing with the time of the end, and from the hand also a faire signe after to appeare.

And here so much for parallizing of this expensive time, with that time of wantonnesse, in his reigne not found currant. In which want none found: of weakenesse, willfulnesse begetting, lifted up like the empty Scale, when the full descends: The Sunne like at lowest, making then the longest shaddow. Thus represented in this Mirror of former times, the present age the visage thereof, &c. Also, no spare body, unwildy growne and great, every way dangerous division therby unable to stand upon the feete: Not spared by Her, whose song the Worlds farwell these. Disburthened in this ensuing briefe. And plaine to bee in undoing this knot too, the Iron-age done, finished, although this peece difficult to digest, somewhat, &c.

Thou sawest, till that a Stone was cut out without hands, &c.

The summe of these words signifie, the Burthen of Gods word in the last dayes, of a truth disclosing the time of the end. And of premisses the conclusion following: So unexpected Iudgements foretold from them: Also made evident the end of time. Here Stone sharpening Iron, and striking fire, High favours (for the most part) not without a heavie hand imparted: like Jacob and his Brother, the unlike twinnes begotten, or the Blessing in one hand, a Rod of correction in the other, and of which fire already kindled, loving Kindnesse and Iudgement, going hand in hand together, the evill times but touched onely.

Thou sawest, till that a Stone was cut out without hands, which smote the Image.

The Signe in the feete; So in these last dayes: see here, and behold fulfilled, how that very saying:

Thou sawest till that, &c.

By Thee beheld, as much to say, to read a certain Manuscript, the weighty Stone become a Booke, not waiting long for Priviledge,

Imprinted, howsoever soone after.

Certainly; in what yeare testifying the Worlds disolution, Manifested with a heavie one: In the yeare One thousand six hundred twentie five.

That great Plague yeare, out of Darknesse, when the Visions translated of the Man, greatly beloved *Danjell*. For the great dayes breaking forth, cleared those clowdy Characters: As delivered not without a token, since made good, the Brittle standing of his owne Kingdomes, dedicated to the *King* of Great *Brittaine*, Defendor of the Faith.

And of whose making to justifie here, by whom Published; though hitherto by authority with-stood.

Eleanor Audeley, handmayden of the most high *God* of Heaven, this Booke brought forth by Her, fifth Daughter of *George*, Lord of *Castlehaven*, Lord *Avdley*, and Tuitchet. *No* inferior *Peere* of this Land, in Ireland the fifth *Earle*.

Which name blotted a House or Castle, of late fallen by the ancient of dayes: His Kingdomes misteries displaying, nor chosen any obscure Motto. God hath devided thy Kingdome, and numbred, &c.

And farther, of this Stone; of the Builders cast aside: the Summe of this Booke or Subject, besides the day of Iudgement revealed, even that Some standing here, shall not tast of Death, till they see that day. Herewith fell upon the *Roman-Empires* disolation. The World, the great *Man*: the disolution ushered with *Germanies* overthrw unexpecting: As moreover one last serving these Feete, great Brittaines foote too, and Germanie divided both betweene two opinions, Religions, and Buisnesses, where never since a Nation such distractions. For Plagues and greivances, such inward and outward ones, striving to outstrip one another.

Heere-withall foreshewed, the Furious Progresse of the French and Spannish Forces, with those Leagues not in force now. Notwithstanding corsse Marriages, &c. never before so.

The Kings of the North, by those France signified: Likewise the Kings of the South, the *Avstrian* Family, these like whirlwinds tossing the World up and downe from this side to that, &c *and* for the shutting up of this Treatise, lastly; with a Salutation concluded for the Son of Peace, if he had been there saluted, &c.

And at that time shall *Michael* stand up, the great Prince, &c.

Angel land, or *Englands-Iland*, therefore the Arch-angels Name; here the halfe name and abbreviated words, the age or time shortned betokning, &c. And for future things derided their Musique. Daniels. Prophesie shut up prohibited, this time of trouble, their's come to passe notwithstanding. So passing or poasting to the time, at last of deliverance, the blessed resurrection. Heere unfolded that treble or threefold Coard, not easily broken nor altred: Sworne with a high hand, that meeting a Trienniall &c.

For a time and times, and halfe, (or part) from the halfe of Seaven, the hand pointing at the seaventeenth-hundred yeare: That very time, about the halfe but fulfilled of the last Centerie, as five hundred yeares filling up a Period. Lastly, given under the hand lifted up, even five thousand yeares compleate for the age of the World. The Worlds Ages too, parted into three parts, allotted two thousand yeares a peece, or thereabouts. The shortest lot drawne last, for a time and times, and halfe; shortned in the behalfe of His Elect.

From Adam unto Abraham, (offering of his sonne) the first Stage or time; so unto Jerusalems destruction the second. And the last or third, to the end of the World, the glorious Resurrection, &c. And yet farther, for the fortunate figure of five, (Blessed is he that waites and comes) &c. Here two hundred and ninety, and three hundred and five and thirty, amounting to six hundred twentie-five, signifying thereby, the yeare wherein unsealed the Booke of the Prophet Daniell, 1625. and 17. yeares current, sithence a time and times and halfe Likewise, this Bookes Resurrection-time also appointed, waiting for the appeasing neere of these stormes and troubles, a Peaceable time: God was not in the Wind, not in the

Earthquake, not in the Fire: after the fire, at last, the small still voyce. *and* so finished this Booke. (Beyond expectation,) but so came to Passe in the yeare aforesaid, 1625. Shee awakened by a voyce from *Heaeun*, in the *Fifth* moneth, the 28. of July, early in the Morning, the Heavenly voice uttering these words.

There is Ninteene yeares and a halfe to the day of Judgement, and you as the meek Virgin.

These sealed with Virgins state in the Resurrection, when they not giving in Marriage.

And to take heede of Pride, or to that effect spoken or added: But as for the Golden number that heeded well or heard: the cleare voice of a Trumpet inclining thereto; and like the chaffe of the Summer-threshing-flowre scattered. When the Cittie flying or fled from the Pestilence, that Sommers great Visitation, the fifth monethes Farwell, July 28. the Heavie hand, in that very weeke, as weekely the number certified, five thousand deseased of the Plague: Moreover; the ensuing Weeke, giving up the reckoning more full, the number of the dead, amounting to five thousand five hundred and odd, &c. there stoppt or stay'd immediately, as much to say; but a spanne the Worlds age, graven with that deadly Dart, and never to be forgotten, within few dayes how scarce a token? So suddenly ceasing then.

VERS. 36. This is the dreame, and wee will tell the interpretation thereof before the King: thou art this head of gold.

The Iron touched with the Load-stone, turnes towards the North, Great Brittaines foure Crownes or Kingdomes: This gyant-Image armed at all points, England, Angel-gold fought the first fight, incountred Romes Dragon, put to flight his Angels.

The Reformations Leader, the other inferior Kingdome, France the Breast and Armes of Silver, sometimes subject to this Ilands-Crowne, beares onely the Lilly argent for Armes, &c.

Another third Kingdome bearing, rule over all: of brasse, Scotland; Bell Mettle, the Belly and Thighes, the Breeches to wit, or blessing wrestled for, having shrunck a sinnew, halting too. The fourth kingdome of Iron, the feete Ireland broken in peeces by an army, their old customes turn'd into new Lawes, & divided between two Religions, our Ladies & our Lords at strife together: but Woman, what have we to doe with thee, but Potters earth and myrie clay, but water with wine compaird.

And drawing here to the end, or foote of this Image: The fourh Monarchies heavie estate, & that fourth Kingdome weighed both here together, where Princes and Nobles going a begging: The basse set on Horse-backe commanding, without doubt the Gentiles their returne, to wallow in the mire, or Heathenisine-covetousnes and Idolatry: this massy peece importing and expressing no lesse. And further, the Iron feete as inferring besides Irelands denominations, the names of Ferdinand, by whom the devision of these dayes, left for a Legacie to his heires. Also, of that Arch-engin great peeces, Volues of shot where distance of so many miles, not securing without hands or mercie in a moment. Towers trodden under foot, and Ships as townes broken in peeces: doubtlesse which cruell Invention among Christians, sounding the Alarum of the day of Judgement at hand, by those thunderbolts discharged. And in dayes of old, had the mighty Volumes bin, those of late Imprinted, out of doubt repented they had, But this Joseph they knew not the holy Scripture. So old dayes presedents made for the future, the Fathers as it were laying up for the Children, & more tolerable in the day of Judgement for them, then for these times, and these of that rare Art also of the Presse, as wel as peeces, in an instant performed, drawn within the compasse of this stone, cut out without hands, become a mountain: the Kingdome of heaven at hand, pointing therat to be revealed too.

Lastly, this name of Charles, no small Favourites of the Fisher-man taken in his nets, stooping to his unsavorie toe; so come to the French and Spanish Emperors. And Charles the great, since whose daies, a thousand yeares expired neere: Feete of the longest size, of the Tens. Fowre of his Race succeding in the Westerne Empire, setting in Europes-Ocean that eye of the World, No little one, either the other great toe, Charles the fifth, & of his successors some six of them.

Thus of two thousand and two hundred yeares standing, this great Image; foure stories in height, or a nayle driven to the head: layd upon the Anvill by those, in all Arts so able, that further amplification unnecessary, but commended these.

VERS. 44. And in the daies of these Kings, shall the God of heaven set up a Kingdome, which shall never be destroyed: and the Kingdome shall not be left to other people, it shall break in peeces.

Finally, for a watch word also these, let fall; at the end of twelue monethes, &c. verse, 29 And the end of all these at aimed, either Heavens departing: for without some farther mistery, doubtlesse not. Even the not knowne day and houre, shewed about New-yeares-day, when that good time falling, or twelfe-tyde, there then to watch, as those night-watchers, the happie Shepheard, our example.

And Nebuchadnezer for examples sake too, for the future chastised, by whom an Act published the earth throughout, for those that walke in Pride to beware. And signes and wonders for to observe from above; which some carelesse observing not, othersome not discerning not, as blockish. So this sonne of the Morning, walking in his majestie, the heavie sentence falling, as foretold by the Prophet Daniel, for to avoyd the Tree, whereof the leaves faire, and fruit much; as much to say, a faire Pedigree, Kings and Princes growing thereon. And the axe laid to the trees roote, wherefore to shew mercy at length to the poore: Counseled for lengthning of his well-faire and tranquility; lest of the lash tasting as well as others.

And upon greatnesse, none to presume, this Daniel penning feigned Tragedies, none sets forth plain this great Assiryan how; taking his Sabbaticall progresse. In all hast driven from his privy Chamber, how doing in the fielde open Pennance, also grazing before his Palace, feeds with his fellow Asse: And like Eagles-plumes, those stareing locks of his overgrown; a heavie crowne or capp, to keepe his head from cold. Also Oxens pushing hornes-like, thereto crooked nayles as birds of prey, the inseparable crown and septor so going together: Pride and cruelty here, which Brutish condition before served out, that apprentiship before added excellent Majesty, &c. and Lords seeking to him, constrained to cast those high lookes lower, little dreamed of that estate: sometime who from the Bed to mind calling the grave no doubt, and thoughts in their owne likenes begetting Dreames. By this great Monarch dreamed, thought he saw an Image & a stone of that greatnes, certainly lay thinking, when he gone the way of all flesh, gathered to his fathers, upon some peece in his own likenes some everlasting Monument. From whose sudden awakning and up rising also, the Prophet revealing earthly dominions and Monarches, the heaven therewith passing away in a moment of time, even mortalities change for no other passage this, or place of Scripture. But like these mettels foure, the Elements melting, so live for ever, &c.

Finis.

DANIEL. I end all.

Anne Bradstreet
(c. 1612–1672)

Anne Dudley married Simon Bradstreet in 1628 and the couple emigrated to New England in 1630, joining the congregation that would be led by Cotton Mather beginning in 1633. Bradstreet was a Protestant with leanings we might describe as "puritan" (though this word is so fraught as to be rendered virtually meaningless)—that is, she probably maintained religious views that were deeply grounded in the scriptures and a desire to strip away the pomp and excesses of church ritual and doctrine in order to better focus on the message of Christ, she probably believed strongly in God's divine providence, and she probably felt that humans were weak and corrupt, able to be redeemed not through any amount of prayer or good works but rather only through the grace of Jesus.

Though Bradstreet's father and husband were politically powerful in the colonial state of Massachusetts, Bradstreet herself stayed out of the political realm. Bradstreet's first book of poems, *The Tenth Muse*, was published in London in 1650. A second expanded edition printed posthumously includes the poem below, which did not appear in the 1650 edition.

The Flesh and the Spirit

In secret place where once I stood
Close by the Banks of *Lacrim* flood
I heard two sisters reason on

133

Things that are past, and things to come;
One flesh was call'd, who had her eye
On worldly wealth and vanity;
The other Spirit, who did rear
Her thoughts unto a higher sphere:
Sister, quoth Flesh, what liv'st thou on
Nothing but Meditation?

Doth Contemplation feed thee so
Regardlesly to let earth goe?
Can Speculation satisfy
Notion without Reality?
Dost dream of things beyond the Moon
And dost thou hope to dwell there soon?
Hast treasures there laid up in store
That all in th' world thou count'st but poor
Art fancy sick, or turn'd a Sot
To catch at shadowes which are not?
Come, come, Ile shew unto thy sence,
Industry hath its recompence.
What canst desire, but thou maist see
True substance in variety?
Dost honor like? acquire the same,
As some to their immortal fame:
And trophyes to thy name erect
Which wearing time shall ne're deject.
For riches dost thou long full sore?
Behold enough of precious store.
Earth hath more silver, pearls and gold,
Then eyes can see, or hands can hold.
Affect's thou pleasure? take thy fill,
Earth hath enough of what you will.
Then let not goe, what thou maist find,
For things unknown, only in mind,
Spir. Be still thou unregenerate part,
Disturb no more my setled heart,

For I have vow'd, (and so will doe)
Thee as a foe, still to pursue
And combate with thee will and must,
Untill I see thee laid in th' dust.
Sisters we are, ye twins we be.
Yet deadly feud twixt thee and me;
For from one father are we not,
Thou by old Adam wast begot,
But my arise is from above
Whence my dear father I do love.
Thou speak'st me fair but hat'st me sore,
Thy flatt'ring shews I trust no more.
How oft thy slave, hast thou me made,
when I believ'd, what thou hast said,
And never had more cause of woe
Then when I did what thou bad'st doe.
Ile stop mine ears at these thy charms,
And count them for my deadly harms,
Thy sinfull pleasures I doe hate,
Thy riches are to me no bait,
Thine honors doe, nor will I love;
For my ambition lyes above.
My greatest honor it shall be
When I am victor over thee,
And triumph shall, with laurel head,
When thou my Captive shalt be led,
How I do live, thou need'st not scoff,
For I have meat thou know'st not off;
The hidden Manna I doe eat,
The word of life it is my meat.
My thoughts do yield me more content
Then can thy hours in pleasure spent.

Nor are they shadows which I catch,
Nor fancies vain at which I snatch,
But reach at things that are so high,

Beyond thy dull Capacity;
Eternal substance I do see,
With which inriched I would be:
Mine Eye doth pierce the heavens, and see
What is invisible to thee.
My garments are not silk nor gold,
Nor such like trash which Earth doth hold,
But Royal Robes I shall have on,
More glorious then the glistring Sun;
My Crown not Diamonds, Pearls, and gold,
But such as Angels heads infold.
The City where I hope to dwell,
There's none on Earth can parallel;
The stately Walls both high and strong,
Are made of pretious *Jasper* stone;
The Gates of Pearl, both rich and clear,
And Angels are for Porters there;
The Streets thereof transparent gold,
Such as no Eye did e're behold,
A Chrystal River there doth run,
Which doth proceed from the Lambs Throne:
Of Life, there are the waters sure,
Which shall remain for ever pure,
Nor Sun, nor Moon, they have no need,
For glory doth from God proceed:
No Candle there, nor yet Torch light,
For there shall be no darksome night.
From sickness and infirmity,
For evermore they shall be free,
Nor withering age shall e're come there,
But beauty shall be bright and clear;
This City pure is not for thee,
For things unclean there shall not be:
If I of Heaven may have my fill,
Take thou the world, and all that will.

Margaret Fell Fox
(1614–1702)

Margaret Askew Fell Fox is among the best-known Quaker women writers. She converted to Quakerism in 1652 under the spiritual guidance of George Fox while still married to her husband, Thomas Fell, who was involved in England's judicial and political spheres. Fell did not convert himself, but he was sympathetic to the Quakers and allowed meetings in their home. After her husband passed away, Margaret became more active than ever in the movement, writing letters to Charles II petitioning for relief from religious persecution, and she continued to travel and to support other itinerant missionaries. Margaret Fell married George Fox in 1669, and each continued in their efforts to grow and support the Friends. Prior to her marriage, Fell was imprisoned in Lancaster Castle from 1664 to 1668 for refusing to take the oath of allegiance; as a Quaker, she would swear allegiance only to Christ. While in prison, she wrote her most famous tract, which defends the rights of women to preach and prophesy. The text provides biblical evidence to support the notion that God's light shines in women as well as men. Compare her argument to that of Jarena Lee in this volume.

Womens Speaking Justified, Proved, and Allowed by the Scriptures. Whereas it hath been an Objection in the minds of many, and several times hath been objected by the

Clergy, or Ministers, and others, against Womens speaking in the Church; and so consequently may be taken, that they are condemned for medling in the things of God; the ground of which Objection, is taken from the Apostles words, which he Writ in his first Epistle to the Corinthians, chap. 14. vers. 34, 35. And also what he writ to Timothy in the first Epistle, chap. 2. vers. 11, 12. But how far they wrong the Apostle's intentions in these Scriptures, we shall shew clearly when we come to them in their course and order. But first let me lay down how God himself hath manifested his Will and Mind concerning Women, and unto Women.

And first, When God created Man in his own Image; in the Image of God created he them, Male and Female; and God blessed them; and God said unto them, Be fruitful, and multiply: And God said, Behold, I have given you of every Herb, &c. Gen. 1. Here God joyns them together in his own Image, and makes no such distinctions and differences as men do; for though they be weak, he is strong; and as he said to the Apostle, His Grace is sufficient, and his strength is made manifest in weakness, 2 Cor. 12. 9. And such hath the Lord chosen, even the weak things of the world, to confound the things which are mighty; and things which are despised, hath God chosen, to bring to nought things that are, 1 Cor. 1. And God hath put no such difference between the Male and Female as men would make.

***

Let this Word of the Lord, which was from the beginning, stop the mouths of all that oppose Womens Speaking in the Power of the Lord; for he hath put enmity between the Woman and the Serpent; and if the Seed of the Woman speak not, the Seed of the Serpent speaks; for God hath put enmity between the two Seeds, and it is manifest, that those that speak against the Woman and her Seeds Speaking, speak out of the enmity of the old Serpents Seed; and God hath fulfilled his Word and his Promise, When the fulness of time was

come, he hath sent forth his Son, made of a Woman, made
under the Law, that we might receive the adoption of Sons,
Gal. 4. 4, 5.

Moreover, the Lord is pleased, when he mentions his
Church, to call her by the name of Woman, by his Prophets,
saying, I have called thee as a Woman forsaken, and grieved in
Spirit, and as a Wife of Youth, Isa. 54. Again, How long wilt
thou go about, thou back-sliding Daughter? For the Lord hath
created a new thing in the earth, a Woman shall compass a
Man, Jer. 31. 22. And David, When he was speaking of Christ
and his Church, he saith, The Kings Daughter is all glorious
within, her cloathing is of wrought Gold; she shall be brought
unto the King: with gladness and rejoycing shall they be
brought; they shall enter into the Kings Pallace, Psal. 45. And
also King Solomon in his Song, where he speaks of Christ and
his Church, where she is complaining and calling for Christ, he
saith, If thou knowest not, O thou fairest among women, go
thy way by the footsteps of the Flock, Cant. 1. 8. c. 5. 9. And
John, when he saw the wonder that was in Heaven, he saw a
Woman clothed with the Sun, and the Moon under her feet,
and upon her head a Crown of twelve Stars; and there
appeared another wonder in Heaven, a great red Dragon
stood ready to devour her Child: here the enmity appears that
God put between the Woman and the Dragon, Revelations 12.

Thus much may prove that the Church of Christ is a
Woman, and those that speak against the Womans speaking,
speak against the Church of Christ, and the Seed of the
Woman, which Seed is Christ; that is to say, Those that speak
against the Power of the Lord, and the Spirit of the Lord
speaking in a Woman, simply, by reason of her Sex, or because
she is a Woman, not regarding the Seed, and Spirit, and Power
that speaks in her; such speak against Christ, and his Church,
and are of the Seed of the Serpent, wherein lodgeth the
enmity. And as God the Father made no such difference in
the first Creation, nor never since between the Male and the
Female, but always out of his Mercy and loving kindness, had

regard unto the weak. So also, his Son, Christ Jesus, confirms the same thing; when the Pharisees came to him, and asked him, if it were lawful for a man to put away his Wife? he answered and said unto them, Have you not read, That he that made them in the beginning, made them Male and Female, and said, For this cause shall a Man leave Father and Mother, and shall cleave unto his Wife, and they twain shall be one flesh, wherefore they are no more twain but one flesh; What therefore God hath joyned together, let no Man put asunder, Mat. 19.

Again, Christ Jesus, when he came to the City of Samaria, where Jacobs Well was, where the Woman of Samaria was; you may read, in John 4. how he was pleased to preach the Everlasting Gospel to her; and when the Woman said unto him, I know that when the Messiah cometh, (which is called Christ) when he cometh, he will tell us all things; Jesus saith unto her, I that speak unto thee am he; This is more than ever he said in plain words to Man or Woman (that we read of) before he suffered. Also he said unto Martha, when she said, she knew that her Brother should rise again in the last day, Jesus said unto her, I am the Resurrection and the Life: he that believeth on me, though he were dead, yet shall he live; and whosoever liveth and believeth shall never die. Believest thou this? she answered, Yea Lord, I believe thou art the Christ, the Son of God. Here she manifested her true and saving Faith, which few at that day believed so on him, John 11. 25, 26.

Also that Woman that came unto Jesus with an Alabaster Box of very precious Oyntment, and poured it on his Head as he sat at meat; it's manifested that this Woman knew more of the secret Power and Wisdom of God, then his Disciples did, that were filled with indignation against her; and therefore Jesus saith, Why do ye trouble the Woman? for she hath wrought a good work upon me; Verily, I say unto you, Wheresoever this Gospel shall be preached in the whole World, there shall also this that this Woman hath done, be told for a memorial of her, Matt. 26. Mark 14. 3. Luke saith further, She was a sinner, and that she stood at his feet behind him weeping, and began to wash his feet with her tears, and did wipe them with the hair of her head, and kissed his feet, and annointed them with Oyntment. And when Jesus saw the Heart of the Pharaisee that had bidden him to his house, he took occasion to speak unto Simon, as you may read in Luke 7. and he turned to the Woman, and said, Simon, seest thou this Woman? Thou gavest me no water to my feet; but she hath washed my feet with tears, and wiped them with the hair of her head: Thou gavest me no kiss; but this Woman, since I came in, hath not ceased to kiss my Feet: My Head with Oyl thou didst not annoint; but this Woman hath annointed my Feet with Oyntment: Wherefore I say unto thee, her sins, which are many, are forgiven her, for she hath loved much, Luke 7. 37, to the end.

Also there was many Women which followed Jesus from Galilee, ministring unto him, and stood afar off when he was Crucified, Mat. 28. 55. Mark 15. Yea even the Women of Jerusalem wept for him, insomuch that he said unto them, Weep not for me, ye Daughters of Jerusalem, but weep for your selves, and for your Children, Luke 23. 28.

And certain Women which had been healed of evil Spirits and Infirmities, Mary Magdalen; and Joanna the wife of Chuza, Herods Stewards Wife; and many others which minis-tred unto him of their substance, Luke 8. 2, 3.

Thus we see that Jesus owned the Love and Grace that appeared in Women, and did not despise it; and by what is recorded in the Scriptures, he received as much love, kind-ness, compassion, and tender dealing towards him from Women, as he did from any others, both in his life time, and also after they had exercised their cruelty upon him; for Mary Magdalene, and Mary the Mother of Joses, beheld where he was said; And when the Sabbath was past, Mary Magdalene, and Mary the Mother of James, and Salom, had brought sweet spices that they might annoint him: And very early in the morning, the first day of the week, they came unto the

Sepulchre at the rising of the Sun; And they said among themselves, Who shall roll us away the stone from the door of the Sepulchre? And when they looked, the stone was rolled away, for it was very great; Mark 16. 1, 2, 3, 4. Luke 24. 1, 2. and they went down into the Sepulchre; and as Matthew saith, The Angel rolled away the stone; and he said unto the Women, Fear not, I know whom ye seek, Jesus which was Crucified: he is not here, he is risen, Mat. 28. Now Luke saith thus, That there stood two men by them in shining apparel, and as they were perplexed and afraid, the men said unto them, He is not here; remember how he said unto you when he was in Galilee, That the Son of Man must be delivered into the hands of sinful men, and be crucified, and the third day rise again; and they remembred his words, and returned from the Sepulchre, and told all these things to the eleven, and to all the rest.

It was Mary Magdalene, and Joanna, and Mary the Mother of James, and the other Women that were with them, which told these things to the Apostles, And their words seemed unto them as idle tales, and they believed them not. Mark this, ye despisers of the weakness of Women, and look upon your selves to be so wise; but Christ Jesus doth not so, for he makes use of the weak: for when he met the Women after he was risen, he said unto them, All Hail, and they came and held him by the Feet, and worshipped him; then said Jesus unto them, Be not afraid; go tell my Brethren that they go into Gallilee, and there they shall see me, Mat. 28. 10. Mark 16. 9. And John saith, when Mary was weeping at the Sepulchre, that Jesus said unto her, Woman, why weepest thou? what seekest thou? And when she supposed him to be the Gardiner, Jesus saith unto her, Mary; she turned her self, and saith unto him, Rabboni, which is to say Master; Jesus saith unto her, Touch me not, for I am not yet ascended to my Father, but go to my Brethren, and say unto them, I ascend unto my Father, and your Father, and to my God, and your God, John 20. 16, 17.

Mark this, you that despise and oppose the Message of the Lord God that he sends by Women; what had become of the Redemption of the whole Body of Man-kind, if they had not believed the Message that the Lord Jesus sent by these Women, of and concerning his Resurrection? And if these Women had not thus, out of their tenderness and bowels of love, who had received Mercy, and Grace, and forgiveness of sins, and Virtue, and Healing from him; which many men also had received the like, if their hearts had not been so united and knit unto him in love, that they could not depart as the men did, but sat watching, and waiting, and weeping about the Sepulchre until the time of his Resurrection, and so were ready to carry his Message, as is manifested; else how should his Disciples have known, who were not there?

Oh! blessed and glorified be the Glorious Lord; for this may all the whole body of man-kind say, though the wisdom of man, that never knew God, is alwayes ready to except against the weak; but the weakness of God is stronger then men, and the foolishness of God is wiser then men.

***

And now to the Apostles words, which is the ground of the great Objection against Womens Speaking; And first, 1 Cor. 14. let the Reader seriously read that Chapter, and see the end and drift of the Apostle in speaking these words: for the Apostle is there exhorting the Corinthians unto charity, and to desire Spiritual gifts, and not to speak in an unknown tongue; and not to be Children in understanding, but to be Children in malice, but in understanding to be men; and that the Spirits of the Prophets should be subject to the Prophets; for God is not the Author of Confusion, but of Peace: And then he saith, Let your Women keep silence in the Church, &c.

Where it doth plainly appear that the Women, as well as others, that were among them, were in confusion; for he saith,

How is it Brethren? when ye come together, every one of you
hath a Psalm, hath a Doctrine, hath a Tongue, hath a
Revelation, hath an Interpretation? let all things be done to
edifying. Here was no edifying, but all was in confusion speaking together; Therefore he saith, If any man speak in an
unknown Tongue, let it be by two, or at most by three, and
that by course; and let one Interpret; but if there be no
Interpreter, let him keep silence in the Church. Here the Man
is commanded to keep silence as well as the Woman, when
they are in confusion and out of order.

But the Apostle saith further, They are commanded to be in
Obedience, as also saith the Law; and if they will learn any
thing, let them ask their Husbands at home; for it is a shame
for a Woman to speak in the Church.

Here the Apostle clearly manifests his intent; for he speaks
of Women that were under the Law, and in that Transgression
as Eve was, and such as were to learn, and not to speak pub-
lickly, but they must first ask their Husbands at home; and it
was a shame for such to speak in the Church: And it appears
clearly, that such Women were speaking among the
Corinthians, by the Apostles exhorting them from malice and
strife, and confusion, and he preacheth the Law unto them,
and he saith, in the Law it is written, With men of other
tongues, and other lips, will I speak unto this people, vers. 2.

And what is all this to Womens Speaking? that have the
Everlasting Gospel to preach, and upon whom the Promise of
the Lord is fulfilled, and his Spirit poured upon them according to his Word, Acts 2. 16, 17, 18. And if the Apostle would
have stopped such as had the Spirit of the Lord poured upon
them, why did he say just before, If any thing be revealed to
another that sitteth by, let the first hold his peace? and you
may all prophesie one by one. Here he did not say that such
Women should not Prophesie as had the Revelation and Spirit
of God poured upon them; but their Women that were under
the Law, and in the Transgression, and were in strife, confusion & malice in their speaking; for if he had stopt Womens

praying or prophesying, why doth he say, Every man praying or prophesying, having his head covered, dishonoreth his head; but every Woman that prayeth or prophesieth with her head uncovered, dishonoreth her head? Judge in your selves, Is it comely that a Woman pray or prophesie uncovered? For the Woman is not without the Man, neither is the Man without the Woman, in the Lord, 1 Cor. 11. 3, 4, 13.

Katharine Evans
(c. 1618–1692)

More than any other religious sect that emerged out of
the tumult of the civil war and interregnum, the
Quakers upheld women's abilities to publicly preach
and prophesy. Katharine Evans was a Quaker mission-
ary who traveled, preached, and wrote during and after
the interregnum. Like Margery Kempe, Evans traveled to a number of places throughout the British
kingdom to spread the good news and was repeatedly
arrested, whipped, and banished. In 1658, she and fellow Quaker Sarah Cheevers were traveling to
Alexandria by way of Malta. They never made it to
their destination. Evans and Cheevers were imprisoned by the Maltese inquisition until 1662, when powerful and sympathetic intercessors successfully
negotiated their release. The text that Evans wrote
during this time is part travel and captivity narrative,
part spiritual autobiography and statement of Quaker
beliefs. The selection below is a powerful statement of
the Quaker belief that, "There is *something* of God in
everyone," and that the truth and the light are attain-
able by all.

There is *something* of God in every one, that would receive
Gods truth if it should; but all that is not of God in every one
doth strive and fight against it, and doth persecute and
imprison till death Gods Messengers, which he hath endued
with power from on high, and hath given them gifts and

graces, and spiritual mercies of divine vertue, to preach to the
Poor and to the captives, to the exiled and banished, and to
sow the seed of Righteousness, that God might receive the
fruits of holiness among his People. *They that sow to the flesh,
do of the flesh reap corruption; but they that sow to the Spirit,
do of the Spirit reap Life everlasting.*

They that have not received the Spirit, they cannot sow to
the Spirit; but they that have received, they sow to the Spirit,
and do profit the people, where they come to be received, and
they do bring forth fruits of God-like lives, and righteous conversations, and heavenly behavior, and their fruits do manifest
what ministry they are under; as St. *Paul* said, *You are our
Epistles written in our hearts, seen and read of all men.* A pure
life and a holy conversation is a sure evidence of a true
Christian, and a perfect witness that they have received the
Spirit of Christ, which maketh a Christian, and generateth into
his body; *Christ the Head, and Christians the Members;* and
he will not have any deformed member in his body, but they
must be all compleat in Christ, *Pure, as he is Pure; Holy, as he
is Holy; Undefiled, as he is Undefiled:* even so as he is, so must
his be in this present world; *He that sanctifieth, and they that
are sanctified, are all one,* as saith the Scriptures: But I say, in
the Name and Power of the pure and perfect Lord God, *That
whosoever, or whatsoever he is in this world that taketh upon
himself, or goeth about to make Christians, or convert Souls
any other way, than by preaching the immediate Word of God
as he doth receive it by the Inspiration of the eternal Spirit of
Life and Power, he is in the highest degree of Presumption, and
guilty of the great Transgression, and shall assuredly receive
the greatest Condemnation from the Lord God of Power, if
they or he do not speedily repent and forsake those great
Abominations.*

Me thinks, that every rational and soberminded Man, must
needs rightly understand, that God Almighty, who created all
them, at the beginning, in Heaven, Earth, and Sea, without
the help or advice of any, and doth uphold the Works of his

own Creation by the Word of his Power; and as he created the
Souls and Minds of men in a pure State of Innocency, from
whence man fell through Disobedience.

So he it is alone, that can, and will, and doth quicken the
Souls of men and women again, and create them anew, in
Christ Jesus, the Lord from heaven, the second *Adam*, a
quickening Spirit, the *Immanuel* of Eternal Life, of the Word
of his Power; and need not the Assistance or Counsel of any
besides himself, to raise up Souls to life and immortality; for
our God is an invisible, eternal, and immortal Spirit, perfect,
holy, wise and powerful: and every reasonable man must
needs know, and believe, That there is not any thing, but only
a Spirit, that can so much as touch a Soul as to cleanse it, or
to defile it; so it is the unrighteous spirit of Darkness, the
Prince of the Power of the Air, that doth rule in the Children
of Disobedience, and polluteth the Souls, and defileth the
whole Minds, and causeth them to yield up the fleshly
Members, to commit sins of all kinds, in Thought, Word and
Action; and so the Springs of Life and Salvation are dammed
up, and the pure Spirit of the Lord is covered, and the Eye of
Innocency blinded, so that man cannot behold his Maker,
because Sin hath made a separation, as saith the Prophet,
*Behold the Lord's hand is not shortned, that it cannot save;
neither is his eare heavy, that he cannot hear; but it is your
iniquities that have separated between you and your God, and
your sins have caused his face to be hid from you:* And as it is
the unclean Spirit that doth defile and pollute the Mind and
Soul, and corrupt the Heart of man; hence it is that nothing
but the clean and pure Spirit of the Lord God, that can in any
wise cleanse and sanctifie the Soul and Mind, or purge, or
purifie the Heart again: and it seems to be a very vain thing
for any man or woman to think otherwise. Now let every one
that is called a Minister of Jesus Christ, see that he be so
indeed and in truth; for they must come a great way before
they can administer Christ: Wherefore it is safe to consider,
that Death reigned, or reigneth, from *Adam* to *Moses*, and

from *Moses* till the Prophet *John;* and *John* was a burning & a shining Light, the greatest that was born among women; *but the least in the Kingdom of God is greater than he:* and *John* cried in the Wilderness, saying, *Prepare ye the Way of the Lord, make his Paths streight;* for he, whose shooe he was not worthy to unloose, was coming after him, *whose fan is in his hand, and he will throughly purge his Floor, and gather the Wheat into the Garner; but the Chaff he will burn with Fire unquenchable.* And *John* denied not, and said, *He was not that Light, but he came to bear witness of the Light,* saying, *This is the true Light, that lighteth every one that cometh into the world.* Now it behoveth all that are called Ministers of Christ, to call themselves to mind how they travelled through all these Administrations, spiritually, from *Adam* till *Moses,* ye are all in death; and when you have received the just and holy Law of *Moses* upon *Mount Sinai,* then you must journey through all the Prophesies, till you come to *Mount Sion,* the heavenly *Jerusalem,* the City of the living God, before you can be a noble Minister of Jesus Christ: And this I am bold to declare in the Name of the Lord Jesus, whose Servant I am through mercy. Be ye not deceived, the Lord God will not be mocked any longer; there is a great Mystery in Godliness, insomuch, that all the earthly Wisdom, and Learning, and Languages, Studies or Prudency is never able to fathom or comprehend the least Motion of the Life of it; but as the Mind is joyned to the Light, the Word of Life, the Word that was before the World was, the Word by which the World was made, the Word that is quick and powerful, sharper than a two-edged Sword, even to the piercing and dividing between soul and spirit, joynts and marrow, and is a searcher and dis-cerner of the Thoughts and Intents of every ones heart; and this is he, whose Vesture is dipt in Blood; his Name is called the Word of God, and he is come according to the determi-nate Counsel of the Father, to make a separation between the Pretious and the Vile, and to divide the Sheep from the Goats, and to gather in the Flock of his Inheritance, the People of his own Pasture, the Sheep of his hands, to fill up his own Fold, out of every Kindred, Tongue and Nation, *Jew and Gentile*, Bond or Free, of his Israelites indeed, in whose mouths there is no guile; and he will place his Name amongst them again, and work his Fear in their hearts, and write his Laws in their inward-parts, that they may never depart from it; and they shall be his People for ever, and he will be their God eternally, and he will be merciful to their Transgressions; their Sins and Iniquities he will remember no more; for our God cannot deny himself, nor forget his holy Promises, who hath said, *I have given Him for a Covenant of Light, to enlighten the* Gentiles, *and a Leader, and Commander to the people:* and the day is come, that all the Children of the Lord shall be taught of the Lord, and be established in Righteousness. And as for those Ministers that say, Men and women can never be freed from Sin, while they are here, nor made perfect while they are in the body; I say, such Ministers do not know Christ Jesus the Light, nor his Ministry, which saith, *When he ascended up on High, he led Captivity captive, & gave gifts unto men; some Prophets, some Apostles, some Ministers, for the perfecting of the Saints, and for the Work of the Ministry, and for the edifying of the whole body of the Church.* And again it is said, *All Scripture given by the Inspiration of the Holy Ghost, is wholsome for Doctrine, for Instruction, for Reproof, and Correction in Righteousness, that the man of God may be made perfect, and thorowly furnished to every good Work.*

Mary Cary
(c. 1620–unknown)

Whereas much is known about the prophetess Eleanor
Davies, the historical record tells little about the life of
Mary Cary. Judging by her written work, she was educated, and she was a millenarian, like Anna Trapnel,
anticipating the imminent reign of Jesus to begin. She
was part of the millenarian community that included
Christopher Feake, Henry Jesse, and Hugh Peter,
male spiritual leaders by whose testimony the work of
several female prophets was authorized. Like Davies's,
Cary's prophetic tracts draw on the biblical texts of
Daniel and Revelation to illuminate contemporary
political and religious affairs. The text below describes
the raising of the New Model Army as the resurrection
of the two witnesses of Revelation. Footnotes to the
selection are Cary's; original spellings and punctuations
are preserved from the 1648 text.

To the Reader. Our Lord Jesus Christ, in the eighteenth
Chapter of *Luke*, from the first to the eighth verse, from the
example of the importunate widdow, stirring up his Disciples
to importunate praier, he there assures them, That God will
surely hear the praiers of his own elect that cry to him day and
night, and avenge them of their adversaries; and this he will
doe for them, though he make them tarry long. And hereby
Saints may be assured, That God will hear their frequent
importunate praiers, which night and day they have put up
against the man of sinne, the Beast, and their Babylonian

enemies, who have troden the Saints under feet, and made
warre against them, and overcome them, and dealt cruelly
with them above this twelve hundred years: and that he will at
last avenge them on these their enemies. But saies our Savior
at the eighth verse, *Neverthelesse, when the Sonne of man
cometh, shall he finde faith on earth?* Whereby he implies,
That when hee cometh, his people shall scarce have faith to
beleeve that hee will thus avenge them on their enemies. But
when he shall come to doe it, it will be beyond their faith. And
even thus is it with Saints now, they have scarce faith to
believe, that the Lord Jesus hath now begun, and is going on
to avenge his own elect on their adversaries, the mysticall
Babylonians. Now for the strengthening of the faith of Saints
concerning this thing, I doe present them with this ensuing
Discourse, wherein as the Lord hath discovered it to me (to
the strengthening of my faith concerning the prosperity of
Sion henceforward, and giving me great joy and pleasure
therein). I have made it to appeare from the Scriptures, That
the Lord hath already lifted up his Saints from under the vas-
salage of their enemies, and hath begunne to put the cup of
trembling, into the hands of them that afflicted them. Which
I desire that all that love, and honour the Lord Jesus may diligently observe.

For the most high God, of whom, and through whom, and to
whom are all things, and for whose pleasure they are, and
were created, both whose wisdome and knowledge are
unfathomable; tels his people of old by the Prophet Isaiah, as
wee have it in the fourty eighth Chapter of his Prophesie, at
the third and the fifth verses, That he declared from the
beginning the things hee would bring to passe, and that he
shewed it them before it came to passe: and he gives the reason why he did so, in the fourth and fifth verses, *Because* (said
hee) *I knew that thou art obstinate, and thy necke is an iron
sinew, and thy brow brasse: And, least thou shouldest say,
Mine idol hath done them, and my graven image, and my*

molten image hath commanded them. And therefore the
Prophet Isaiah in the fourty eighth Chapter, and fourteenth
verse, hee makes a challenge to the Nations, and to the
People, to assemble themselves, and to shew which among
them hath declared those things. But there is none to be
found among the sonnes of men that can declare any thing:
for he maketh the diviners mad, &c. And *Isaiah* the fourty
third, and the thirteenth, he saith, *Before the day was, I am
hee, and there is none that can deliver out of mine hands: I
will work, and who shall let it.* And *Isaiah* the fourtie six
Chapter, and the ninth and tenth verses, *I am God, and there
is none like mee, Declaring the end from the beginning, and
from ancient times, the things that are not yet done, saying,
My counsell shall stand, and I will doe all my pleasure.* And
yet notwithstanding all this, that people of *Israel*, who had
seene and knowne, (or might have) all the glorious workes of
the most high, and observed how he declared things before
they came to passe, and had thereby a greater advantage then
the Heathen, of being convinced of his eternall Power and
God-head: Yet were they so vile, as to question it, having in
them an emnitie to the true God, and chose rather to worship
Idols, and denie the Eternall God: As appeares in the fourty
sixth Chapter of *Isaiah*, and therefore at the eighth and ninth
verses, he saies, *Remember this, and shew your selves men,
and bring it againe to minde, O yee transgressours. Remember
the former things of old, for I am* GOD, *and there is none else,
I am* GOD, *and there is none like me, Declaring the end from
the beginning, and from ancient times the things that are not
yet done; saying, My counsell shall stand, and I will doe all my
pleasure.* Remember; as if hee had said, and shew your selves
men, shew your selves to be rationall creatures, and be not as
the horse and mule that hath no understanding; but seeing I
have declared from ancient times, the things I would doe long
before they came to passe: saying, My counsell shall stand,
and I will doe all my pleasure: And be ye thereby convinced,
that I am GOD, and there is none like me. But as then, so now,

are there many that are become Atheists, denying the true
GOD, and JESUS CHRIST, whom he hath sent, whose necke are
an iron sinew, and their brow brasse, who had they not lost
the principles of reason, might by the things of the Creation,
be convinced of his Eternall Power and God-head, *Romans*
the first Chapter, and the twentieth verse. As also by observing how hee declared, what it was his will to bring to passe
long agoe, and how hee hath brought to passe what hee so
declared. But they have lost even the principles of reason
which they once had, by which they might have then been
convinced hereof; whereby they are left without excuse, as
the Apostle saies, *Romans* the first and the twentieth. But
they having lost reason, are now become vaine in their imagi-
nations, and their foolish heart is darkened; and though they
professe themselves to be wise, and are puft up with selfe-
conceits of wisdome, in their frothy and blasphemous
Discourses: yet they are become fooles, changing the truth of
GOD into a lie. And the Apostle gives the reason why GOD hath
thus given them over, in the first Chapter to the Romans the
one and twentieth, and the eight and twentieth verses,
Because they did not like to retaine GOD in their knowledge,
and because that when they knew GOD, they glorified him not
as GOD. The like reason hee giveth, why them that perish are
deceived by the man of sinne, as in the second Epistle to the
Thessalonians the second Chapter, and the tenth verse,
Because they received not the love of the truth.

But now, Though Atheists, and Papists, denie the Eternall
GOD, and observe not his wonderfull workes, how he declares
things long before they come to passe: saying, My counsell
shall stand, and I will doe all my pleasure; and accordingly
brings it to passe, because their foolish heart is darkned: yet
all his Saints doe, and will observe this: For saith the Psalmist,
in the hundred and eleventh *Psalme*, and the second and third
verses, *The workes of the LORD are great, sought out of all*
them that have pleasure therein. His worke is honourable, and

glorious, and his righteousnesse endureth for ever: He hath made his wonderfull workes to be remembred, &c. The LORD hath made his wonderfull workes to be remembred among his Saints, though others remember them not, yet his Saints have pleasure in them, and therefore search them out, and they have a promise made to them, That in the observing the wonderfull things of the LORD, they shall understand his loving kindenesse, it runnes thus, *Who so is wise, and will observe these things, even they shall understand the loving kindenesse of the LORD,*[1] as Psalme the hundred and third and the fourty third verse. Now it being so, let Saints diligently observe the ensuing Discourse, wherin it doth appear, That GOD hath brought to passe the things he did fifteen hundred yeares agoe predeclare; which they observing it may tend much to the strengthening of their faith in this, That JESUS CHRIST hath begun, and is going on to avenge them on their enemies. For in the ensuing Discourse it will appear, That as JESUS CHRIST did long since reveale to *John,* how that after the mysticall Babylonians had persecuted his Saints a long time, he would raise up his Saints out of their persecuted condition, and bring down those their *Babylonian* enemies: So hee hath alreadie begunne to doe this thing, even to raise up his Saints, and to bring downe their enemies, and that punctually, according to what hee did reveal to *John.*

---

[1] *The Psalmist in the former part of that Psalme, had been speaking of severall passages of the providence of GOD, which it concerns the Saints to observe, amongst the rest these are some,* he poureth contempt upon Princes, causeth them to wander in the wildernesse where there is no way; yet he sitteth the poor on high from affliction, and maketh him families like a flock. The righteous shall see it and rejoice, and all iniquity shall stop her mouth. Now this is that which is by the Saints to be observed at this time also, *even how GOD beginneth to pour contempt upon Babylonish princes, viz., Bishops and other Babylonian [Factours?], and to set the Saints that were looked upon as poor despised ensuing creatures on high from affliction and to make of them families like a flock, who not long since were small in number, but now is this number greatly increased.*

Now I know there hath been observed by many Saints, many things that GOD revealed to *John*, which he hath brought to passe. Many of which Observations are already in print: but that which I chiefly aim at in this Discourse, is that which is not yet printed by any other, and whether any other have yet observed it, I know not; but they are passages so eminently worthy to be observed, in this present time, because they give the Saints such ground of encouragement and consolation, in respect of the happy successe that shall be of the very present affairs of this Kingdome (how knotty and difficult so ever for the present, or for sometime, yet they may appear to be) as that in love to all Saints I could not but communicate them to them in this way.

But there are two things, which it may be may cause some to retain some unbeleeving and doubtfull thoughts concerning the happy successe of present things, although it be made clear in the following Discourse, That the time of Saints being cloathed in sackcloth is expired.

First, It may be some cannot receive it, because they look for farther judgements to come upon this Kingdome, (wherein outwardly the Saints may suffer also) because of the great provoking sins of this Kingdom, as drunkennesse, and adulteries, and oaths, and their entering into so many Covenants concerning religious things, for which they have no sufficient warrant, now in the times of the Gospel, and the oppressions of the poor, and meaner sort of people, and the great neglect of doing justice generally, &c. Now to these I say, That it is true, that if God should deal with this Nation, according to its demerits; then indeed no other could be expected, but an utter desolation of it, that it might either swim in bloud, or burn with fire untill it were consumed. But

First, I desire you to consider, That God hath a very great number of his dear Saints in this Kingdom, in whom he delights, and for whose sake he may, and I had almost said, will spare this Kingdome, and spare the Cities and Towns, and Counties where they are for if God would have spared *Sodome* for ten righteous persons, we have a great ground of hope, that he will spare *London*, yea all *England* from a generall devastation and desolation, having thousands of righteous persons in *London*, and in all *England* a very great number. And how many plots of wicked men, wherein they endeavored the ruine of this Kingdome, hath God blasted? Having such a great number of his precious jewels in it.

And secondly, What though here be in this Kingdome, many that are great enemies to Jesus Christ, yet God can by his Covenant of Grace, bring many of them in to the obedience of Christ, and make them of persecutors to become eminent Saints, and call those his people that were not his people: And why should we doubt whether he would do so, since these are the times wherein he hath promised to do so, and hath already begun to doe it? But

Thirdly, If it be so, that some are hardned to destruction, and they are never quiet, but still are plotting against the just, to ruine them: yet know they shall not prevail over the Saints, but in opposing them shall ruine themselves, *Zech*. 12. 3. as appears in the following Discourse.

Secondly, Doubtfull thoughts may be in others, that yet the Saints may be overcome, because they see they have so many enemies abroad, and at home, and they are speaking great words, and are still plotting against them. To such, I say, Let them suppose that there were none that did dare to make any opposition at all in this Kingdome, but that all things went smoothly on, in the hands of those that are carrying it on: and if they could then beleeve, that indeed God would not have his Saints in this Kingdome to be troden under foot by the Beast any more. Then let them have the same faith to beleeve it now, as knowing it is as easie with God, to carry on this work over the mountains as over the plains, and he will make the great mountain to become a plain before Zerubbabel, before his people, Zech. 4. 7. He can command those that are preparing warre against them to sit still, and proceed no farther, and put a fear upon them; or if they doe goe on, yet he can make it to come to nothing, and to be the most effectual way to lay them lower, and to raise his people higher.

Now if any particular man would be as sure of safety, as all the Witnesses in generall are; then if he be a man in any pub-like imploiment, let him according to his place oppose the Beast, and act for the welfare of all that wish well to Sion, and doe justice unto all, from the highest unto the lowest, and be more forward to act for the meanest, then for the highest. Let him suppose the condition of the meanest man[1] that seeks to him for just things to be his own condition, and act for him, as hee would be dealt with himself were he in that condition: for thus relieving of the poor and distressed ones, is most accept-able to the Lord of Sabbath, and in so doing, I am confident it will go well with him, however it go with others.

Again, If he be a private man; let him also in his place, wish well to Sion, and oppose the Beast; so shall he also prosper in the prosperity of Sion.

And now Reader, who ever thou art, if thou dost receive any benefit of any kinde, by reading the ensuing Discourse, whether of encouragement, consolation, information, or quickning, I beseech thee to return all the glory of it to the most High, to whom alone it is due, who for that end made use of so weak an instrument: in whom if thou be a friend to the Lord Jesus Christ, I am

Thy friend
[&]
serve thee
M. Cary.

---

[1] *I say, for those that seek for just things, not for those that seek for unjust things, as for protection in evil waies or places of profit or honour, when they neither deserve them nor are fit for them, or else have too many already, &c.*

Anna Trapnel
(fl. 1642–1660)

During the civil war and interregnum in England
(1642–1660), many emergent religious sects became
hopeful that the deposing of King Charles I (whose
Catholic sympathies, political gaffes, and exorbitant
spending had made him exceedingly unpopular, to the
extent that some equated him with the Antichrist)
would usher in a new era of religious freedom. Some of
the faithful even believed the millennial reign of Jesus
was at hand. Anna Trapnel was one such millenarian. A
Baptist and Fifth Monarchist, Trapnel's prophetic
utterances were both spiritual and political. She saw
Oliver Cromwell initially as a Gideon who would usher
in Christ's reign; when he became Lord Protector, she
prophesied against him, saying that though there was a
new title, Cromwell was no better than the kings of old.
"Hannah Trapnel" was known by the Cromwellian government; Marchamont Needham, part of Cromwell's
political circle, observed her and attested to her ability
to draw and influence a crowd. She was arrested and
imprisoned in 1654, as she recounts in another narrative. Trapnel was one of many women prophets and
preachers who attained agency and authority in the
early modern public sphere.

The passage below comes from her major prophetic, political tract, *The Cry of a Stone*, in which she
establishes her prophetic voice and, through an anony-
mous relator, describes her experiences and visions.

Spelling and punctuation from the 1654 text are preserved in the excerpts below.

I am *Anna Trapnel*, the daughter of *William Trapnel*,
Shipwright, who lived in *Poplar*, in *Stepney* Parish; my father
and mother living and dying in the profession of the Lord
Jesus: my mother died nine years ago, the last words she
uttered upon her death-bed, were these to the Lord for her
daughter. Lord! Double thy spirit upon my child; these words
she uttered with much eagerness three times, and spoke no
more; I was trained up to my book and writing, I have walked
in fellowship with the Church meeting at *All-hallows*, (whereof
Mr. *John Simpson* is a Member) for the space of about four
years; I am well known to him and that whole Society, also to
Mr. *Greenhil* Preacher at Stepney, and most of that society, to
Mr. *Henry Jesse*, and most of his society, to Mr. *Venning*
Preacher at *Olaves* in *Southwark*, and most of his society, to
Mr. *Knollis*, and most of his society, who have knowledge of
me, and of my conversation; If any desire to be satisfied of it,
they can give testimony of me, and of my walking in times
past.

Seven years ago I being visited with a feaver, given over by
all for dead, the Lord then gave me faith to believe from that
Scripture. After two days I will revive thee, the third day I will
raise thee up, and thou shalt live in my sight: which two days
were two weeks that I should lye in that feaver, and that very
time that it took me, that very hour it should leave me, and I
should rise and walk, which was accordingly: From this time,
for a while year after, the Lord made use of me for the
refreshing of the afflicted and tempted ones, inwardly and
outwardly. And when that time was ended; I being in my
Chamber, desired of the Lord to tell me whether I had done
that which was of and from himself. Reply was, thou shalt
approve thy heart to God, and in that thou hast been faithfull
in a little, I make thee an Instrument of much more; for particular souls shall not only have benefit by thee, but the

universality of Saints shall have discoveries of God through thee: So upon this I prayed that I might be led by the still waters, and honor God secretly, being conscious to my self of my own evil heart, looking upon my self as the worst of all God's flock; the Lord upon it told me, that he would out of the mouth of babes and sucklings perfect his praise; then I remained silent, waiting with prayer and fasting, with many tears before the Lord for whole Sion: And upon that day called Whitson-Monday, which was suddenly after, I finding my heart in a very low dead frame, much contention and crookedness working in my Spirit; I asked God what was the matter, he answered me thus; I let thee see what thou are in thy self to keep thee humble, I am about to shew thee great things and visions which thou hast been Ignorant of: I being thus drawn into my Chamber: after this there was a day of thanksgiving that I kept with the Church of *All-hallows* in *Limestreet*, for the Army that was then drawing up towards the City, in which I had a little discovery of the presence of the Lord with them, in which day I had a glorious Vision of the New Jerusalem, which melted me into rivers of tears, that I shrunk down in the room; and cryed out in my heart, Lord, what is this? it was answered me, A discovery of the glorious state of whole Sion, in the raign of the Lord Jesus, in the midst of them, and of it thou shalt have more visions hereafter; So then when the day was ended, I retired to my Chamber, at that time living in the Minories in *Aldgate* Parish, where I conversed with God by prayer, and reading of the Scriptures, which were excellently opened to me touching the Proceedings of the Army.

It was first said to me that they were drawing up toward the City (I not knowing any thing of it before) and that there was a great hubbub in the City, the shops commanded to be shut up; Upon this I went down, and enquired of the maid of the house, whether there was any stir in the City; She answered me, you confine your self to your Chamber, and take no notice of what is done abroad; We are commanded, said she, to shut up our shops, and there are great fears amongst the Citizens; what will be the issue, they know not; With that I answered, blessed be the Lord that hath made it known to so low a servant as I; Then repairing to my Chamber again, I looked out at the window, where I saw a flag at the end of the street; this word I have presently upon it, thou seest that flag, the flag of defiance is with the Army, the King of *Salem* is on their side, he marcheth before them, he is the Captain of their Salvation; At the other end of the street, I looking, saw a hill (it was *Black-heath*) it was said to me, thou seest that hill, not one but many hills rising up against *Hermonhill*, They shall fall down and become Vallies before it: It was then said unto me, Go into the City, and see what is done there: where I saw various things from the Lord in Order to his appearance with the Army; as I was going, hearing of a Trumpeter say to a Citizen these words, we have many Consultations about one coming up but nothing yet goes on, presently it was said to me, the Councels of men shall fall, but the Councel of the Lord stands sure, and his works shall prosper: So repairing home, I had many Visions, that the Lord was doing great things for this Nation . . .

❖❖❖

Upon the Tenth day of the Eleventh Moneth, 1653. The Relator coming into the Chamber where she lay, heard her first making Melody with a spiritual Song, which he could not take in but part, and that too with such imperfection, as he cannot present any account of it to the understanding of others: After her Song, she without intermission uttered forth her Spirit in prayer, wherein among many other, she expressed the passages following.

What is marvelous or can be in the eyes of the Lord? the resurrection of Jesus was marvelous in our eyes, but not with the Lord, for nothing could keep down a Jesus; thy people could never have come out of their graves, had it not been for

the Resurrection of Jesus; as thou risedst, so should they, as
thou dyedst, so should they, thou wilt make all things death
before them; what endeavorings were there to have kept thee
in the Grave? oh, but what fastness, what locks, what bolts
that could keep in a Jesus? oh, but they thought that the Lord
Jesus was but a man, they understood not that the Divine
Nature was wrapt up in him in the Humane Nature; when thy
time came the Sepulchre was open, and the Lord Jesus came
forth with great Power and Majesty; oh blessed be the Lord
that brought forth the Son, the Heir, him that was victorious
over his enemies; so shall there be a Declaration against all
things that would keep thine down; faith is that victory; how
so? because faith brings into the bosom, and it draws forth the
Death and Resurrection of Jesus upon us: thou art a bringing
forth a great resurrection: Jesus Christ is upon his appearing;
there are some do think so, but they say it is not yet begun,
God will bring it about another way, and another time; but the
Lord says, he will cut short his work in Righteousness; thou
knowest who are the *Babylonians* that are now about thine; as
thou didst to thy people of Old, thou will come forth speedily,—thy thoughts are so exceeding high and glorious that
none is able to reach them; Man cannot bring forth his own
thoughts, they are so tumultuous, and run unto the ends of the
Earth; oh then what are thy thoughts O Lord,—though the
Enemy begin to jeer them concerning those blessed songs;
well says God, are my people jeered concerning their
Excellencies, their Songs, their *Hallelujahs* that are of my own
making, that are before my throne? the Lord cannot endure
that these Excellencies of his Saints should be trampled upon,
which are so perfect, so pure; how pleasant are the songs of
thine, when they are brought forth out of the Churches of
thine Enemies.—Tis not all the force in the world that can
strike one stroak against thine, but thou sufferest them to
come forth to try thine; oh that thine could believe thee for
thy breakings of them, as well as for thy bindings up; all things
under the Sun, all things before you, in you, shall work for

your good; when they come to understand more of the mystery, and of the entrals of Scripture, how will they praise thy Highness? The Enemies are strong, Satan is strong, Instruments are strong, Temptations they are strong, what Strengths are against thy flock! They cannot be without the Lyon, and Lyon-like creatures: Oh if thy Servants suffer, let them not suffer for passion or rash words, but as Lambs; there is a zeal which is but from Nature, a mans own spirit may prompt him to, but the zeal of God is accompanied with meekness, humility, grief for Christ.—Since thy Handmaid is taken up to walk with thee, thy Handmaid always desired that she might be swift to hear, slow to speak; but now that thou has taken her up into thy Mount, who can keep in the rushing wind? who can bind the influences of the Heavenly Orion, who can stop thy Spirit? It is good to be in the Territories, in the Regions, where thou walkest before thy Servant; oh how glittering, and how glorious are they, what Sparklings are there!—Thou hast a great gust to come upon the Earth, a great wind that shall shake the trees that now appear upon the Earth, that are full of leaves of Profession; but they have nothing but outward beauty, an outward flourish; but thy trees O Lord, they are full of Sap: A great number of people said, oh let our Oaks stand, let them not be cut down: oh but says the Lord, I will make you ashamed in the Oaks that you have chosen; and because you will have these Oaks, I will now give you other Oaks, and what are they? A first, a second and a third Power, and thou breakest them one after another; oh thine own have had a great hand in these things; thine have said, we will have Oaks and Gardens, but how have they run too and fro! says the Lord now, I will give you Gardens; but they shall have no springs in them, they shall be as dry chapt ground, they shall be as fallow ground: what loveliness is there to walk upon fallow ground? you shall have stumbling walkings upon them, you shall have no green grass in these Gardens; what have all the Gardens of the Earth been? they have been to thine places of stumbling: O thou wilt by these thy strange ways, draw up thine into thy upper and nether springs: thou hast deceived thy Saints once again about these Gardens: let them now run after them no more, but be ashamed and abashed: we have hankered from mountain to hill, we have said salvation is in this hill and in that, but let us say so no longer: when we shall thus be drawn up to thee, then we shall prosper, and thou wilt give us Vineyards, and Gardens, and Trees of thine own, which shall abide.—Thou calledst thy servant to come sometimes near this place, to witness against some, who said that the Kingdom was already given up to the Father, and contemned the Man Christ; but now hast thou sent thy Servant again to witness for thee, for the Kingdom of thy Son.

Phillis Wheatley
(c. 1753–1784)

Phillis Wheatley was born in Africa, perhaps in Senegal
or Gambia, and brought to New England on a slave
ship when she was just a child. In 1761, she was pur-
chased by Susannah Wheatley in Boston. Phillis was a
precocious child who learned quickly and whose
accomplishments won her the admiration and attention of her owners. Although she was a slave, the
Wheatleys oversaw her education, which included les-
sons in Latin and English literature. Under the patron-
age of the countess of Huntingdon, who was acquainted
with the Wheatleys, Phillis's book of poems was published in 1773. The book has numerous prefatory
epistles from prominent Boston citizens attesting to
the quality, authenticity, and attribution of the work.
Phillis gained greater entrée into Boston society such
that she was able to buy her freedom, and became
known even to George Washington for whom she
wrote a poem in 1775. The poem below displays her
talents, especially the extent to which she could
manipulate traditional poetic forms.

Thoughts on the Works of Providence

Arise, my soul, on wings enraptured rise,
To praise the monarch of the earth and skies,
Whose goodness and beneficence appear
As round its center moves the rolling year,

Or when the morning glows with rosy charms,
Or the sun slumbers in the ocean's arms;
Of light divine be a rich portion lent,
To guide my soul and favor my intent.
Celestial muse, my arduous flight sustain,
And raise my mind to a seraphic strain.

Adored forever be the God unseen,
Which round the sun revolves this vast machine,
Though to his eye its mass a point appears;
Ador'd the God that whirls surrounding spheres,
Which first ordained that mighty *Sol* should reign,
The peerless monarch of th' ethereal train;
Of miles twice forty millions is his height,
And yet his radiance dazzles mortal sight,
So far beneath—from him th' extended earth
Vigor derives, and ev'ry flow'ry birth;
Vast through her orb she moves with easy grace.
Around her *Phoebus* in unbounded space;
True to her course th' impetuous storm derides,
Triumphant o'er the winds and surging tides.

Almighty, in these wondrous works of thine,
What *Pow'r*, what *Wisdom* and what *Goodness* shine!
And are thy wonders, Lord, by men explor'd,
And yet creating glory unador'd!

Creation smiles in various beauty gay,
While day to night, and day succeeds to day;
That *Wisdom* which attends *Jehovah's* ways,
Shines most conspicuous in the solar rays;
Without them, destitute of heat and light,
This world would be the reign of endless night;
In their excess how would our race complain,
Abhorring life! how hate its lengthen'd chain!
From air a-dust what num'rous ills would rise

What dire contagion taint the burning skies?
What pestilential vapors, fraught with death,
Would rise and overspread the lands beneath!

Hail, smiling morn, that from the orient main
Ascending dost adorn the heavenly plain!
So rich, so various are thy beauteous dyes,
That spread through all the circuit of the skies,
That, full of Thee, my soul in rapture soars,
And thy great God, the cause of all adores.

O'er beings infinite His love extends,
His *Wisdom,* rules them, and His Pow'r defends,
When talks diurnal tire the human frame,
The spirits faint, and dim the vital flame,
Then too that ever active bounty shines,
Which not infinity of space confines.
The sable veil, that *Night* in silence draws,
Conceals effects, but shows th' *Almighty Cause;*
Night seals in sleep the wide creation fair,
And all is peaceful but the brow of care.
Again, gay *Phoebus* as the day before,
Wakes ev'ry eye, but what shall wake no more;
Again the face of nature is renew'd,
Which still appears harmonious, fair and good.
May grateful strains salute the smiling morn,
Before its beams the eastern hills adorn!

Shall day to day, and night to night, conspire
To show the goodness of the Almighty sire?
This mental voice shall man, regardless, hear,
And never, never raise the filial prayer?
Today, O hearken, nor your folly mourn
For time misspent, that never will return.

But see the sons of vegetation rise,
And spread their leafy banners to the skies.
Allwise, Almighty Providence we trace

In trees, and plants, and all the flow'ry race;
As clear as in the nobler frame of man,
All lovely copies of the Maker's plan.
Th' pow'r the same that forms a ray of light,
That call'd creation from eternal night.
"Let there be light," He said: from His profound
Old *Chaos* heard, and trembled at the sound:
Swift as the word, inspir'd by pow'r divine,
Behold the light around its Maker shine,
The first fair product of th' omnisic God,
And now through all his works diffus'd abroad.

As reason's pow'rs by day our God disclose,
So may we trace him in the nights repose!
Say, what is sleep? and dreams, how passing strange!
When action ceases, and the ideas range
Licentious and unbounded o'r the plains,
Where *Fancy's* queen in giddy triumph reigns.
Hear, in soft strains, the dreaming lover sigh
To a kind fair, or rave in jealousy;
On pleasure now, and now on vengeance bent,
The lab'ring passions struggle for a vent.
What pow'r, O man! thy reason then restores,
So long suspended in nocturnal hours!
What secret hand returns the mental train,
And gives, improv'd, thine active pow'rs a gain?
From thee, O man, what gratitude should rise!
And when from balmy sleep thou op'st thine eyes,
Let thy first thoughts be praises to the skies.
How merciful our God who thus imparts
O'erflowing tides of joy to human hearts,
When wants and woes might be our righteous lot,
Our God forgetting by our God forgot!

Among the mental pow'rs a question rose,
"What most the image of th' Eternal shows?"
When thus to *Reason* (so let *Fancy* rove)

Her great companion spoke immortal *Love*.

"Say mighty pow'r, how long shall strife prevail,
"And with its murmurs load the whisp'ring gale?
"Refer the cause to *Recollection's* shrine,
"Who loud proclaims my origin divine,
"The cause whence heav'n and earth began to be,
"And is not man immortalized by me?
"Reason let this most ceaseless strife subside."
Thus *Love* pronounced and *Reason* thus reply'd:

"Thy birth, celestial queen! 'tis mine to own,"
"In thee resplendent is the God-head shown;
"Thy words persuade, my soul enraptur'd feels,
"Resistless beauty which thy smile reveals."
Ardent she spoke, and, kindling at her charms,
She clasp'd the blooming goddess in her arms.

Infinite *Love* where'er we turn our eyes
Appears: This ev'ry creature's wants supplies;
This most is heard in Nature's constant voice,
This makes the morn, and this the eve rejoice;
This bids the fost'ring rains and dews descend
To nourish all, to serve one general end,
The good of man: yet man ungrateful pays
But little homage, and but little praise,
To Him, whose works array'd with mercy shine,
What songs should rise, how constant, how divine!

Jarena Lee
(1783–unknown)

Like other women in this volume, including Margery
Kempe and Katharine Evans, Jarena Lee was an itinerant woman preacher. She traveled and spread her spiritual message, eventually publishing an account of her
experiences. Jarena Lee was the first woman preacher
in the African Methodist Episcopalian (AME) church.
Her preaching was approved of and encouraged by her
Bishop, Richard Allen. The first selection below
records his reaction and her thoughts about the first
time she approached Allen regarding her vocation;
compare, for example, to Fell Fox's *Women's Speaking
Justified*. The second recounts Lee's marriage and her
time in the community where her husband preached.

My Call to Preach the Gospel. Between four and five years
after my sanctifications, on a certain time, an impressive
silence fell upon me, and I stood as if some one was about to
speak to me, yet I had no such thought in my heart.—But to
my utter surprise there seemed to sound a voice which I
thought I distinctly heard, and most certainly understand,
which said to me, "Go preach the Gospel!" I immediately
replied aloud, "No one will believe me." Again I listened, and
again the same voice seemed to say—"Preach the Gospel; I
will put words in your mouth, and will turn your enemies to
become your friends."

At first I supposed that Satan had spoken to me, for I had
read that he could transform himself into an angel of light for

171

the purpose of deception. Immediately I went into a secret place, and called upon the Lord to know if he had called me to preach, and whether I was deceived or not; when there appeared to my view the form and figure of a pulpit, with a Bible lying thereon, the back of which was presented to me as plainly as if it had been a literal fact.

In consequence of this, my mind became so exercised, that during the night following, I took a text and preached in my sleep. I thought there stood before me a great multitude, while I expounded to them the things of religion. So violent were my exertions and so loud were my exclamations, that I awoke from the sound of my own voice, which also awoke the family of the house where I resided. Two days after I went to see the preacher in charge of the African Society, who was the Rev. Richard Allen, the same before named in these pages, to tell him that I felt it my duty to preach the gospel. But as I drew near the street in which his house was, which was in the city of Philadelphia, my courage began to fail me; so terrible did the cross appear, it seemed that I should not be able to bear it. Previous to my setting out to go to see him, so agitated was my mind, that my appetite for my daily food failed me entirely. Several times on my way there, I turned back again; but as often I felt my strength again renewed, and I soon found that the nearer I approached to the house of the minister, the less was my fear. Accordingly, as soon as I came to the door, my fears subsided, the cross was removed, all things appeared pleasant—I was tranquil.

I now told him, that the Lord had revealed it to me, that I must preach the gospel. He replied, by asking, in what sphere I wished to move in? I said, among the Methodists. He then replied, that a Mrs. Cook, a Methodist lady, had also some time before requested the same privilege; who, it was believed, had done much good in the way of exhortation, and holding prayer meetings; and who had been permitted to do so by the verbal license of the preacher in charge at the time. But as to women preaching, he said that our Discipline knew

nothing at all about it—that it did not call for women preachers. This I was glad to hear, because it removed the fear of the
cross—but no sooner did this feeling cross my mind, than I
found that a love of souls had in a measure departed from me;
that holy energy which burned within me, as a fire, began to
be smothered. This I soon perceived.

O how careful ought we to be, lest through our by-laws of
church government and discipline, we bring into disrepute
even the word of life. For as unseemly as it may appear now-
a-days for a woman to preach, it should be remembered that
nothing is impossible with God.

And why should it be thought impossible, heterodox, or
improper for a woman to preach? seeing the Savior died for
the woman as well as for the man.

If the man may preach, because the Savior died for him,
why not the woman? seeing he died for her also. Is he not a
whole Savior, instead of a half one? as those who hold it wrong
for a woman to preach, would seem to make it appear.

Did not Mary *first* preach the risen Savior, and is not the
doctrine of the resurrection the very climax of Christianity—
hangs not all our hope on this, as argued by St. Paul? Then did
not Mary, a woman, preach the gospel? for she preached the
resurrection of the crucified Son of God.

But some will say that Mary did not expound the Scripture,
therefore, she did not preach, in the proper sense of the term.
To this I reply, it may be that the term preach in those primi-
tive times, did not mean exactly what it is now made to mean;
perhaps it was a great deal more simple then, than it is now—
if it were not, the unlearned fishermen could not have
preached the gospel at all, as they had no learning.

To this it may be replied, by those who are determined not
to believe that it is right for a woman to preach, that the disciples, though they were fishermen and ignorant of letters too,
were inspired so to do. To which I would reply, that though
they were inspired, yet that inspiration did not save them from
showing their ignorance of letters, and of man's wisdom; this

the multitude soon found out, by listening to the remarks of the envious Jewish priests. If then, to preach the gospel, by the gift of heaven, comes by inspiration solely, is God straitened; must he take the man exclusively? May he not, did he not, and can he not inspire a female to preach the simple story of the birth, life, death, and resurrection of our Lord, and accompany it too with power to the sinner's heart. As for me, I am fully persuaded that the Lord called me to labor, according to what I have received, in his vineyard. If he has not, how could he consistently bear testimony in favor of my poor labors, in awakening and converting sinners?

In my wanderings up and down among men, preaching according to my ability, I have frequently found families who told me that they had not for several years been to a meeting, and yet, while listening to hear what God would say by his poor female instrument, have believed with trembling—tears rolling down their cheeks, the signs of contrition and repentance towards God. I firmly believe that I have sown seed, in the name of the Lord, which shall appear with its increase at the great day of accounts, when Christ shall come to make up his jewels.

At a certain time, I was beset with the idea, that soon or late I should fall from grace and lose my soul at last, I was frequently called to the throne of grace about this matter, but found no relief; the temptation pursued me still. Being more and more afflicted with it, till at a certain time, when the spirit strongly impressed it on my mind to enter into my closet and carry my case once more to the Lord; the Lord enabled me to draw nigh to him, and to his mercy seat, at this time, in an extraordinary manner; for while I wrestled with him for the victory over this disposition to doubt whether I should persevere, there appeared a form of fire, about the size of a man's hand, as I was on my knees; at the same moment there appeared to the eye of faith a man robed in a white garment, from the shoulders down to the feet; from him a voice proceeded, saying: "Thou shalt never return

from the cross." Since that time I have never doubted, but
believe that God will keep me until the day of redemption.
Now I could adopt the very language of St. Paul, and say that
nothing could have separated me from the love of God,
which is in Christ Jesus. Since that time, 1807, until the present, 1833, I have not even doubted the power and goodness
of God to keep me from falling, through the sanctification of
the spirit and belief of the truth.

My Marriage. In the year 1811, I changed my situation in
life, having married Mr. Joseph Lee, pastor of a Society at
Snow Hill, about six miles from the city of Philadelphia. It
became necessary therefore for me to remove. This was a
great trial at first, as I knew no person at Snow Hill, except my
husband, and to leave my associates in the society, and especially those who composed the *band* of which I was one. None
but those who have been in sweet fellowship with such as
really love God, and have together drank bliss and happiness
from the same fountain, can tell how dear such company is,
and how hard it is to part from them.

At Snow Hill, as was feared, I never found that agreement
and closeness in communion and fellowship, that I had in
Philadelphia, among my young companions, nor ought I to
have expected it. The manners and customs at this place were
somewhat different, on which account I became discontented
in the course of a year, and began to importune my husband
to remove to the city. But this plan did not suit him, as he was
the Pastor of the Society, he could not bring his mind to leave
them. This afflicted me a little. But the Lord showed me in a
dream what his will was concerning this matter.

I dreamed that as I was walking on the summit of a beautiful hill, that I saw near me a flock of sheep, fair and white, as
if but newly washed; when there came walking toward me a
man of a grave and dignified countenance, dressed entirely in
white, as it were in a robe, and looking at me, said emphati-
cally, "Joseph Lee mast take care of these sheep, or the wolf

will come and devour them." When I awoke I was convinced
of my error, and immediately, with a glad heart, yielded to the
right spirit in the Lord. This also greatly strengthened my
faith in his care over them, for fear the wolf should by some
means take any of them away. The following verse was beautifully suited to our condition, as well as to all the little flocks of
God scattered up and down this land:

> "Us into Thy protection take,
> And gather with Thine arm;
> Unless the fold we first forsake
> The wolf can never harm."

After this, I fell into a state of general debility, and in an ill
state of health, so much so, that I could not sit up; but a desire
to warn sinners to flee the wrath to come, burned vehemently
in my heart, when the Lord would send sinners into the house
to see me. Such opportunities I embraced to press home on
their consciences the things of eternity, and so effectual was
the word of exhortation made through the Spirit, that I have
seen them fall to the floor crying aloud for mercy.

From this sickness I did not expect to recover, and there
was but one thing which bound me to earth, and this was, that
I had not as yet preached the gospel to the fallen sons and
daughters of Adam's race, to the satisfaction of my mind. I
wished to go from one end of the earth to the other, crying,
Behold, behold the lamb! To this end I earnestly prayed the
Lord to raise me up, if consistent with his will. He conde-
scended to hear my prayer, and to give me a token in a dream,
that in due time I should recover my health. The dream was
as follows: I thought I saw the sun rise in the morning, and
ascend to an altitude of about half an hour high, and then
become obscured by a dense black cloud, which continued to
hide its rays for about one-third part of the day, and then it
burst forth again with renewed splendor.

This dream I interpreted to signify my early life, my conversion to God, and this sickness, which was a great affliction, as

it hindered me, and I feared would forever hinder me from preaching the gospel, was signified by the cloud; and the bursting forth of the sun, again, was the recovery of my health, and being permitted to preach.

I went to the throne of grace on this subject, where the Lord made this impressive reply in my heart, while on my knees: "Ye shall be restored to thy health again, and worship God in full purpose of heart."

This manifestation was so impressive, that I could but hide my face as if some one was gazing upon me, to think of the great goodness of the Almighty God to my poor soul and body. From that very time I began to gain strength of body and mind, glory to God in the highest, until my health was fully recovered.

For six years from this time I continued to receive from above, such baptisms of the Spirit as mortality could scarcely bear. About that time I was called to suffer in my family, by death—five, in the course of about six years, fell by his hand; my husband being one of the number, which was the greatest affliction of all.

I was now left alone in the world, with two infant children, one of the age of about two years, the other six months, with no other dependence than the promise of Him who hath said—I will be the widow's God, and a father to the fatherless. Accordingly, he raised me up friends, whose liberality comforted and solaced me in my state of widowhood and sorrows, I could sing with the greatest propriety the words of the Poet.

> "He helps the stranger in distress,
> The widow and the fatherless,
> And grants the prisoner sweet release."

I can say even now, with the Psalmist, "Once I was young, but now I am old, yet I have never seen the righteous forsaken, nor his seed begging bread." I have ever been fed by his beauty, clothed by his mercy, comforted and healed when sick, succored when tempted, and every where upheld by his hand.

Maria W. Stewart
(1803–1879)

Maria W. Stewart occupied many important roles: political activist, speaker, writer, abolitionist, feminist, and spiritual leader. Her parents were free blacks; however, they passed away when she was only five. She became a servant in a minister's household, where she received no education. As a young adult, Stewart sought education at Sabbath schools, and she quickly caught up, becoming extremely literate and articulate, as her sophisticated work suggests. Married briefly to James Stewart, Maria became a widow in 1829, after only three years. She focused her energies on giving speeches and writing on abolition and the rights of women, particularly black women. The selection below comes from Stewart's *Meditations*, the first edition of which was published in 1832.

Prayer. . . . I have been taking a survey of the American people in my own mind, and I see them thriving in arts, and sciences, and in polite literature. Their highest aim is to excel in political, moral, and religious improvement. They early consecrate their children to God, and their youth indeed are blushing in artless innocence; they wipe the tears from the orphan's eyes, and they cause the widow's heart to sing for joy; and their poorest ones, who have the least wish to excel, they promote. And those that have but one talent, they encourage. But how very few are there among them that bestow one thought upon the benighted sons and daughters of Africa,

who have enriched the soils of America with their tears and
blood; few to promote their cause, none to encourage their
talents. Under these circumstances, do not let our hearts be
any longer discouraged; it is no use to murmur nor to repine,
but let us promote ourselves and improve our own talents.
And I am rejoiced to reflect that there are many able and tal-
ented ones among us whose names might be recorded on the
bright annals of fame. But, "*I can't*," is a great barrier in the
way. I hope it will soon be removed, and "*I will*," resume its
place.

***

Righteousness exalteth a nation, but sin is a reproach to any
people. Why is it, my friends, that our minds have been
blinded by ignorance to the present moment? 'Tis on account
of sin. Why is it that our church is involved in so much difficulty? It is on account of sin. Why is it that God has cut down,
upon our right hand and upon our left the most learned and
intelligent of our men? O, shall I say, it is on account of sin!
Why is it that thick darkness is mantled upon every brow, and
we, as it were, look sadly upon one another? It is on account
of sin. O, then, let us bow before the Lord our God, with all
our hearts, and humble our very souls in the dust before him;
sprinkle, as it were, ashes upon our heads, and awake to righteousness, and sin not. The arm of the Lord is not shortened,
that it cannot save; neither is his ear heavy, that he cannot
hear; but it is your iniquities that have separated you from me,
saith the Lord. Return, O ye backsliding children, and I will
return unto you, and ye shall be my people, and I will be your
God.

O, ye mothers, what a responsibility rests on you! You have
souls committed to your charge, and God will require a strict
account of you. It is you that must create in the minds of your
little girls and boys a thirst for knowledge, the love of virtue,
the abhorrence of vice, and the cultivation of a pure heart.

The seeds thus sown will grow with their growing years; and the love of virtue thus early formed in the soul will protect their inexperienced feet from many dangers. O, do not say, you cannot make anything of your children; but say, with the help and assistance of God, we will try. Do not indulge them in their little stubborn ways; for a child left to himself bringeth his mother to shame. Spare not, for their crying; thou shall beat them with a rod and they shall not die; and thou shall save their souls from hell. When you correct them, do it in the fear of God, and for their own good. They will not thank you for your false and foolish indulgence; they will rise up, as it were, and curse you in this world; and, in the world to come, condemn you. It is no use to say, you can't do this, or, you can't do that: you will not tell your Maker so, when you meet him at the great day of account. And you must be careful that you set an example worthy of following, for you they will imitate. There are many instances, even among us now, where parents have discharged their duty faithfully, and their children now reflect honor upon their gray hairs.

Perhaps you will say, that many parents have set pure examples at home, and they have not followed them. True, our expectations are often blasted; but let us not dishearten you. If they have faithfully discharged their duty, even after they are dead, their works may live; their prodigal children may then return to God, and become heirs of salvation; if not, their children cannot rise and condemn them at the awful bar of God.

Perhaps you will say, that you cannot send them to high schools and academies. You can have them taught in the first rudiments of useful knowledge, and then you can have private teachers, who will instruct in the higher branches: and their intelligence will become greater than ours, and their children will attain to higher advantages, and *their* children still higher; and then, though we are dead, our works shall live; though we are moldering, our names shall not be forgotten.

Finally, my heart's desire and prayer to God is, that there might come a thorough reformation among us. Our minds have too long groveled in ignorance and sin. Come, let us incline our ears to wisdom, and apply our hearts to understanding; promote her, and she shall exalt thee; she shall bring thee to honor when thou dost embrace her. An ornament of grace shall she be to thy head, and a crown of glory shall she deliver to thee. Take fast hold of instruction; let her not go; keep her, for she is thy life. Come, let us turn unto the Lord our God, with all our heart and soul, and put away every unclean and unholy thing from among us, and walk before the Lord our God, with a perfect heart, all the days of our lives; then we shall be a people with whom God shall delight to dwell; yea, we shall be that happy people whose God is the Lord.

I am of a strong opinion, that the day on which we unite, heart and soul, and turn our attention to knowledge and improvement, that day the hissing and reproach among the nations of the earth against us will cease. And even those who now point at us with the finger of scorn, will aid and befriend us. It is of no use for us to sit with our hands folded, hanging our heads like bulrushes, lamenting our wretched condition; but let us make a mighty effort, and arise; and if no one will promote or respect us, let us promote and respect ourselves.

The American ladies have the honor conferred on them, that by prudence and economy in their domestic concerns, and their unwearied attention in forming the minds and manners of their children, they laid the foundation of their becoming what they now are. The good women of Wotliersfied, Conn., toiled in the blazing sun, year after year, weeding onions, then sold the seed and procured money enough to erect them a house of worship; and shall we not imitate their examples, as far as they are worthy of imitation? Why cannot we do something to distinguish ourselves, and contribute some of our hard earnings that would reflect honor upon our memories, and cause our children to arise and call us blessed? Shall it any longer be said of the daughters of Africa, they have no ambition, they have no force? By no means. Let every female heart become united and let us raise a fund ourselves; and at the end of one year and a half, we might be able to lay the corner-stone for the building of a High School, that the higher branches of knowledge might be enjoyed by us; and God would raise us up, and enough to aid us in our laudable designs. Let each one strive to excel in good housewifery, knowing that prudence and economy are the road to wealth. Let us not say, we know this, or, we know that, and practice nothing; but let us practice what we do know.

How long shall the fair daughters of Africa be compelled to bury their minds and talents beneath a load of iron pots and kettles? Until union, knowledge, and love begin to flow among us. How long shall a mean set of men flatter us with their smiles, and enrich themselves with our hard earnings; their wives' fingers sparkling with rings, and they themselves laughing at our folly? Until we begin to promote and patronize each other. Shall we be a mere by-word among the nations any longer? Shall they laugh us to scorn forever? Do you ask, what can we do? Unite and build a store of your own, if you cannot procure a license. Fill one side with dry-goods and the other with groceries. Do you ask, where is the money? We have spent more than enough for nonsense to do what building we should want. We have never had an opportunity of displaying our talents; therefore the world thinks we know nothing. And we have been possessed of by far too mean and cowardly a disposition, though I highly disapprove of an insolent or impertinent one. Do you ask the disposition I would have you possess? Possess the spirit of independence. The Americans do, and why should not you? Possess the spirit of men, bold and enterprising, fearless and undaunted. Sue for your rights and privileges. Know the reason that you cannot attain them. Weary them with your importunities. You can but die, if you make the attempt; and we shall certainly die if you do not. The Americans have practiced nothing but head-work these 200 years, and we have done their drudgery. And is it not high time for us to imitate their examples, and practice head-work too, and keep what we have got, and get what we can? We need never to think that anybody is going to feel interested for us, if we do not feel interested for ourselves. That day we, as a people, hearken unto the voice of the Lord our God, and walk in his ways and ordinances, and become distinguished for our ease, elegance, and grace, combined with other virtues—that day the Lord will raise us up, and enough to aid and befriend us, and we shall begin to flourish.

***

Were every gentleman in America to realize as one that they had got to become bondmen, and their wives, their sons, and their daughters, servants forever to Great Britain, like Belshazzar, their joints would become loosened, and tremblingly would smite one against another; their countenance would be filled with horror, every nerve and muscle would be forced into action; their souls would recoil at the very thought, their hearts would die within them, and death would be far more preferable. Then why have not Afric's sons a right to feel the same? Are not their wives, their sons, and their daughters as dear to them as those of the white man's? Certainly God has not deprived them of the divine influences of his Holy Spirit, which is the greatest of all blessings, if they ask him. Then why should man any longer deprive his fellow man of equal rights and privileges? O, America, America, foul and indelible is thy stain! Dark and dismal is the cloud that hangs over thee for thy cruel wrongs and injuries to the fallen sons of Africa. The blood of her murdered ones cries to heaven for vengeance against thee. Thou art almost become drunken with the blood of her slain; thou hast enriched thyself through her toils and labors; and now thou refuseth to make even a small return. And thou hast caused the daughters of Africa to commit whordoms and fornications; but upon thee be their curse.

O, ye great and mighty men of America, ye rich and powerful ones, many of you will call for the rocks and mountains to fall upon you, and to hide you from the wrath of the lamb, and from him that siteth upon the throne; whilst many of the sable-skinned Africans you now despise, will shine in the kingdom of heaven as the stars, forever and ever. Charity begins at home, and those that provide not for their own, are worse than infidels. We know that you are raising contributions to aid the gallant Poles; we know that you have befriended Greece and Ireland; and you have rejoiced with France for her heroic deeds of valor. You have acknowledged all the nations of the earth, except Hayti; and you may publish, as far as the East is from the West, that you have two millions of negroes, who aspire no higher than to bow at your feet and to court your smiles. You may kill, tyrannize and oppress as much as you choose, until our cry shall come up before the throne of God; for I am firmly persuaded that he will not suffer you to quell the proud, fearless and undaunted spirit of the Africans forever; for in his own time, he is able to plead his own cause against you, and to pour out upon you the ten plagues of Egypt. We will not come out against you with swords and staves, as against a thief; but we will tell you that our souls are fired with the same love of liberty and independence with which your souls are fired. We will tell you that too much of your blood flows in our veins, and too much of your color in our skins, for us not to possess your spirits. We will tell you that it is our gold that clothes you in fine linen and purple, and causes you to fare sumptuously every day; and it is the blood of our fathers and the tears of our brethren that have enriched your soils. *And we claim our rights*. We will tell you that we are not afraid of them that kill the body, and after that can do no more; but we will tell you whom we do fear. We fear Him who is able, after he hath killed, to destroy both soul and body in hell forever. Then, my brethren, sheath your swords, and calm your angry passions. Stand still, and know that the Lord he is God. Vengeance is his, and he will repay. It is a long lane that has no turn. America has risen to her meridian. When you begin to thrive, she will begin to fall. God hath raised you up a Walker and a Garrison. Though Walker sleeps, yet he lives, and his name shall be held in everlasting remembrance. I, even I, who am but a child, inexperienced to any of you, am a living witness to testify unto you this day, that I have seen the wicked in great power, spreading himself like a green bay tree, and lo, he passed away; yea, I diligently sought him, but he could not be found; and it is God alone that has inspired my heart to feel for Afric's woes. Then fret not yourself because of evil doers. Fret not yourself because of the men who bring wicked devices to pass, for they shall be cut down as the grass, and wither as the green herb. Trust in the Lord, and do good; so shalt thou dwell in the land, and verily thou shalt be fed. Encourage the noble-hearted Garrison. Prove to the world that you are neither ourang-outangs, nor a species of mere animals, but that you possess the same powers of intellect as those of the proud-boasting American.

I am sensible, my brethren and friends, that many of you have been deprived of advantages, kept in utter ignorance, and that your minds are now darkened; and if any of you have attempted to aspire after high and noble enterprises, you have met with so much opposition that your souls have become discouraged. For this very cause a few of us have ventured to expose our lives in your behalf, to plead your cause against the great; and it will be of no use, unless you feel for yourselves and your little ones, and exhibit the spirits of men. O, then, turn your attention to knowledge and improvement; for knowledge is power. And God is able to fill you with wisdom and understanding, and to dispel your fears. Arm yourselves with the weapons of prayer. Put your trust in the living God. Persevere strictly in the paths of virtue. Let nothing be lacking on your part, and in God's own time, and his time is certainly the best, he will surely deliver you with a mighty hand and with an outstretched arm.

I have never taken one step, my friends, with a design to raise myself in your esteem or to gain applause. But what I have done has been done with an eye single to the glory of

God, and to promote the good of souls. I have neither kindred nor friends. I stand alone in your midst, exposed to the fiery darts of the devil, and to the assaults of wicked men. But though all the powers of earth and hell were to combine against me, though all nature should sink into decay, still would I trust in the Lord, and joy in the God of salvation. For I am fully persuaded that he will bring me off conqueror; yea, more than conqueror, through him who hath loved me and given himself for me.

Boston, *October*, 1831.

Emily Dickinson
(1830–1886)

Emily Dickinson remained at her family home in Amherst, Massachusetts, for most of her life, a year at Mount Holyoke Seminary and other rare travels excepting. She had few friends; one was the Reverend Charles Wadsworth. Whether the nature of Dickinson's relationship with Wadsworth was romantic has been the matter of some speculation, but there is no conclusive evidence to suggest that it was. Dickinson's writings suggest a shy, sensitive woman who chose a contemplative life. If she had lived in an earlier era, perhaps Dickinson would have been an anchoress like Julian of Norwich. She created a similar isolation in her home, and her poems suggest an emotional distance from other people as much as they reveal moments of inspiration and spiritual communication with the divine. Dickinson's poems, almost 1800 of them, were found after her death; she had collected them into small, hand-bound books which perhaps held some thematic unity.

The following poems are metaphysical. They ruminate upon the divine in the midst of humans' lives and express, in their smallness, the vastness of the deity, the transience of the body, and transcendence of the soul. The first number above each poem shows its place in the source text for these selections. The following number, in parentheses, shows the poem's place in *The Complete Poems of Emily Dickinson*.

259 (625)

'Twas a long Parting—but the time
For Interview—had Come—
Before the Judgment Seat of God—
The last—and second time

These Fleshless Lovers met—
A Heaven in a Gaze—
A Heaven of Heavens—the Privilege
Of one another's Eyes—

No Lifetime—on Them—
Appareled as the new
Unborn—except They had beheld—
Born infiniter—now—

Was Bridal—e'er like This?
A Paradise—the Host—
And Cherubim—and Seraphim—
The unobtrusive Guest—

c. 1862, published 1890.

296 (721)

Behind me—dips Eternity—
Before me—Immortality—
Myself—the Term between—
Death but the drift of Eastern Gray,
Dissolving into Dawn away,
Before the West begin—

'Tis Kingdoms—afterward—they say—
In perfect—pauseless Monarchy—
Whose Prince—is Son of None—
Himself—His Dateless Dynasty—
Himself—Himself diversify—
In Duplicate divine—

'Tis Miracle before Me—then—
'Tis Miracle behind—between—
A Crescent in the Sea—
With Midnight to the North of Her—
And Midnight to the South of Her—
And Maelstrom—in the Sky—

c. 1863, published 1929.

297 (724)

It's easy to invent a Life—
God does it—every Day—
Creation—but the Gambol
Of His Authority—

It's easy to efface it—
The thrifty Deity
Could scarce afford Eternity
To Spontaneity—

The Perished Patterns murmur—
But His Perturbless Plan
Proceed—inserting Here—a Sun—
There—leaving out a Man—

c. 1863, published 1929.

Therèse of Lisieux
(1873–1897)

Therèse was born in Alençon, France, had a powerful conversion experience when she was 14, and joined the Carmelites at Lisieux the following year. Therèse's life was short, only 24 years, but in that time, she dedicated her life to the love of God. Her *Story of a Soul* is a powerful spiritual autobiography, chronicling both dark nights of the soul as well as ecstatic moments of divine inspiration. Her endeavor and her encouragement toward others was to love as a child loves, purely and wholly. She famously fashioned herself as a "little flower of Jesus," an image often attached to her name. Like several other passages in this volume, the one below incorporates imagery from the Song of Songs, but it also bears the kind of optimistic, positive message seen in Julian's description of the "homely" relationship she has with the loving deity, or in Beatrijs of Nazareth's writings on God's love.

Well, I am a child of Holy Church, and the Church is a Queen, because she is now espoused to the Divine King of Kings. I ask not for riches or glory, not even the glory of Heaven that belongs by right to my brothers the Angels and Saints, and my own glory shall be the radiance that streams from the queenly brow of my Mother, the Church. Nay, I ask for Love. To love Thee, Jesus, is now my only desire. Great deeds are not for me; I cannot preach the Gospel or shed my blood. No matter! My brothers work in my stead, and I, a

little child, stay close to the throne, and love Thee for all who
are in the strife.

But how shall I show my love, since love proves itself by
deeds? Well! the little child will strew flowers . . . she will
embalm the Divine Throne with their fragrance, she will sing
Love's Canticle in silvery tones. Yea, my Beloved, it is thus my
short life shall be spent in Thy sight. The only way I have of
proving my love is to strew flowers before Thee that is to say,
I will let no tiny sacrifice pass, no look, no word. I wish to
profit by the smallest actions, and to do them for Love. I wish
to suffer for Love's sake, and for Love's sake even to rejoice:
thus shall I strew flowers. Not one shall I find without scatter-
ing its petals before Thee . . . and I will sing . . . I will sing
always, even if my roses must be gathered from amidst
thorns; and the longer and sharper the thorns, the sweeter
shall be my song.

But of what avail to thee, my Jesus, are my flowers and my
songs? I know it well: this fragrant shower, these delicate petals
of little price, these songs of love from a poor little heart like
mine, will nevertheless be pleasing unto Thee. Trifles they are,
but Thou wilt smile on them. The Church Triumphant, stooping towards her child, will gather up these scattered rose
leaves, and, placing them in Thy Divine Hands, there to
acquire an infinite value, will shower them on the Church
Suffering to extinguish its flames, and on the Church Militant
to obtain its victory.

O my Jesus, I love Thee! I love my Mother, the Church; I
bear in mind that "the least act of pure love is of more value
to her than all other works together."[1]

But is this pure love really in my heart? Are not my boundless desires but dreams but foolishness? If this be so, I
beseech Thee to enlighten me; Thou knowest I seek but the
truth. If my desires be rash, then deliver me from them, and
from this most grievous of all martyrdoms. And yet I confess,

---

[1] St. John of the Cross.

if I reach not those heights to which my soul aspires, this very
martyrdom, this foolishness, will have been sweeter to me
than eternal bliss will be, unless by a miracle Thou shouldst
take from me all memory of the hopes I entertained upon
earth. Jesus, Jesus! if the mere desire of Thy Love awakens
such delight, what will it be to possess it, to enjoy it for ever?

How can a soul so imperfect as mine aspire to the pleni-
tude of Love? What is the key of this mystery? O my only
Friend, why dost Thou not reserve these infinite longings to
lofty souls, to the eagles that soar in the heights? Alas! I am
but a poor little un-fledged bird. I am not an eagle, I have but
the eagle's eyes and heart! Yet, notwithstanding my exceeding
littleness, I dare to gaze upon the Divine Sun of Love, and I
burn to dart upwards unto Him! I would fly, I would imitate
the eagles; but all that I can do is to lift up my little wings—it
is beyond my feeble power to soar. What is to become of me?
Must I die of sorrow because of my helplessness? Oh, no! I
will not even grieve. With daring self-abandonment there will
I remain until death, my gaze fixed upon that Divine Sun.
Nothing shall affright me, nor wind nor rain. And should
impenetrable clouds conceal the Orb of Love, and should I
seem to believe that beyond this life there is darkness only,
that would be the hour of perfect joy, the hour in which to
push my confidence to its uttermost bounds. I should not
dare to detach my gaze, well knowing that beyond the dark
clouds the sweet Sun still shines.

So far, O my God, I understand Thy Love for me. But Thou
knowest how often I forget this, my only care. I stray from Thy
side, and my scarcely fledged wings become draggled in the
muddy pools of earth; then I lament "like a young swallow"[2]
and my lament tells Thee all, and I remember, O Infinite
Mercy! that "Thou didst not come to call the just, but sinners."[3]

[2] Isaiah 38:14.
[3] Matthew 9:15.

Yet shouldst Thou still be deaf to the plaintive cries of Thy feeble creature, shouldst Thou still be veiled, then I am content to remain benumbed with cold, my wings bedraggled, and once more I rejoice in this well-deserved suffering.

O Sun, my only Love, I am happy to feel myself so small, so frail in Thy sunshine, and I am in peace . . . I know that all the eagles of Thy Celestial Court have pity on me, they guard and defend me, they put to flight the vultures the demons that fain would devour me. I fear them not, these demons, I am not destined to be their prey, but the prey of the Divine Eagle.

Eternal Word! O my Savior! Thou art the Divine Eagle Whom I love Who lurest me.

Thou Who, descending to this land of exile, didst will to suffer and to die, in order to bear away the souls of men and plunge them into the very heart of the Blessed Trinity Love's Eternal Home! Thou Who, reascending into inaccessible light, dost still remain concealed here in our vale of tears under the snow-white semblance of the Host, and this, to nourish me with Thine own substance! O Jesus! forgive me if I tell Thee that Thy Love reacheth even unto folly.

And in face of this folly, what wilt Thou, but that my heart leap up to Thee? How could my trust have any limits?

I know that the Saints have made themselves as fools for Thy sake; being eagles, they have done great things. I am too little for great things, and my folly it is to hope that Thy Love accepts me as victim; my folly it is to count on the aid of Angels and Saints, in order that I may fly unto Thee with Thine own wings, O my Divine Eagle! For as long a time as Thou willest I shall remain my eyes fixed upon Thee. I long to be allured by Thy Divine Eyes; I would become Love's prey. I have the hope that Thou wilt one day swoop down upon me, and, bearing me away to the Source of all Love, Thou wilt plunge me at last into that glowing abyss, that I may become for ever its happy Victim.

O Jesus! would that I could tell all little souls of Thine ineffable condescension! I feel that if by any possibility Thou couldst find one weaker than my own, Thou wouldst take delight in loading her with still greater favors, provided that she abandoned herself with entire confidence to Thine Infinite Mercy. But, O my Spouse, why these desires of mine to make known the secrets of Thy Love? Is it not Thyself alone Who hast taught them to me, and canst Thou not unveil them to others? Yea! I know it, and this I implore Thee! . . .

I ENTREAT THEE TO LET THY DIVINE EYES REST UPON A VAST NUMBER OF LITTLE SOULS, I ENTREAT THEE TO CHOOSE, IN THIS WORLD, A LEGION OF LITTLE VICTIMS OF THY LOVE.

Simone Weil
(1909–1943)

Simone Weil was a political activist as well as a Christian
philosopher and mystic. She became the latter under
rather unlikely circumstances, as she was born in an
utterly nonreligious household in France and educated
alongside feminist and existentialist Simone de Beauvoir
at the École Normale Superieure in Paris. She was a
socialist radical, writing and speaking about workers'
rights. She read deeply in philosophy and the world's
religions, and the influence of Eastern thought can be
detected in the selection below as in her other writings.
In 1937 and 1938, Weil had ecstatic religious experiences that marked her conversion. She wrote a spiritual
autobiography, as well as profoundly philosophical
works, including the selection below.

Compare Weil's notion that "If we turn our minds
towards the good, it is impossible that . . . the whole
soul will not be attracted thereto in spite of itself" with
the vision of divine grace penetrating even the recalci-
trant mind described by Hildegard of Bingen earlier in
this volume.

We do not have to understand new things, but by dint of
patience, effort and method to come to understand with our
whole self the truths which are evident.

Stages of belief. The most commonplace truth when it floods
the *whole soul*, is like a revelation.

We have to try to cure our faults by attention and not by will.

The will only controls a few movements of a few muscles, and these movements are associated with the idea of the change of position of nearby objects. I can will to put my hand flat on the table. If inner purity, inspiration or truth of thought were necessarily associated with attitudes of this kind, they might be the object of will. As this is not the case, we can only beg for them. To beg for them is to believe that we have a Father in heaven. Or should we cease to desire them? What could be worse? Inner supplication is the only reasonable way, for it avoids stiffening muscles which have nothing to do with the matter. What could be more stupid than to tighten up our muscles and set our jaws about virtue, or poetry, or the solution of a problem. Attention is something quite different.

Pride is a tightening up of this kind. There is a lack of grace (we can give the word its double meaning here) in the proud man. It is the result of a mistake.

Attention, taken to its highest degree, is the same thing as prayer. It presupposes faith and love.

Absolutely unmixed attention is prayer.

If we turn our minds towards the good, it is impossible that little by little the whole soul will not be attracted thereto in spite of itself.

Extreme attention is what constitutes the creative faculty in man and the only extreme attention is religious. The amount of creative genius in any period is strictly in proportion to the amount of extreme attention and thus is authentic religion at that period.

The wrong way of seeking. The attention fixed on a problem. Another phenomenon due to horror of the void. We do not want to have lost our labor. The heat of the chase. We must not want to find: as in the case of an excessive devotion, we become dependent on the object of our efforts. We need an outward reward which chance sometimes provides and which we are ready to accept at the price of a deformation of the truth.

It is only effort without desire (not attached to an object) which infallibly contains a reward.

To draw back before the object we are pursuing. Only an indirect method is effective. We do nothing if we have not first drawn back.

By pulling at the bunch, we make all the grapes fall to the ground.

There are some kinds of effort which defeat their own object (example: the soured disposition of certain pious females, false asceticism, certain sorts of self-devotion, etc.). Others are always useful, even if they do not meet with success.

How are we to distinguish between them?

Perhaps in this way: some efforts are always accompanied by the (false) negation of our inner wretchedness; with others the attention is continually concentrated on the distance there is between what we are and what we love.

Love is the teacher of gods and men, for no one learns without desiring to learn. Truth is sought not because it is truth but because it is good.

Attention is bound up with desire. Not with the will but with desire—or more exactly, consent.

We liberate energy in ourselves, but it constantly reattaches itself. How are we to liberate it entirely? We have to desire that it should be done in us—to desire it truly—simply to desire it, not to try to accomplish it. For every attempt in that direction is vain and has to be dearly paid for. In such a work all that I call "I" has to be passive. Attention alone—that attention which is so full that the "I" disappears—is required of me. I have to deprive all that I call "I" of the light of my attention and turn it on to that which cannot be conceived.

The capacity to drive a thought away once and for all is the gateway to eternity. The infinite in an instant.

As regards temptations, we must follow the example of the truly chaste woman who, when the seducer speaks to her, makes no answer and pretends not to hear him.

We should be indifferent to good and evil but, when we are indifferent, that is to say when we project the light of our attention equally on both, the good gains the day. This phenomenon comes about automatically. There lies the essential grace. And it is the definition, the criterion of good.

A divine inspiration operates infallibly, irresistibly, if we do not turn away our attention, if we do not refuse it. There is not a choice to be made in its favor, it is enough not to refuse to recognize that it exists.

The attention turned with love towards God (or in a lesser degree, towards anything which is truly beautiful) makes certain things impossible for us. Such is the non-acting action of prayer in the soul. There are ways of behavior which would veil such attention should they be indulged in and which, reciprocally, this attention puts out of the question.

As soon as we have a point of eternity in the soul, we have nothing more to do but to take care of it, for it will grow of itself like a seed. It is necessary to surround it with an armed guard, waiting in stillness, and to nourish it with the contemplation of numbers, of fixed and exact relationships.

We nourish the changeless which is in the soul by the contemplation of that which is unchanging in the body.

Writing is like giving birth: we cannot help making the supreme effort. But we also act in like fashion. I need have no fear of not making the supreme effort—provided only that I am honest with myself and that I pay attention.

The poet produces the beautiful by fixing his attention on something real. It is the same with the act of love. To know that this man who is hungry and thirsty really exists as much as I do—that is enough, the rest follows of itself.

The authentic and pure values—truth, beauty and goodness—in the activity of a human being are the result of one and the same act, a certain application of the full attention to the object.

Teaching should have no aim but to prepare, by training the attention, for the possibility of such an act.

All the other advantages of instruction are without interest.

Studies and faith. Prayer being only attention it is pure form and studies being a form of gymnastics of the attention, school exercise should be a refraction of spiritual life. There must be method in it. A certain way of doing a Latin prose, a certain way of tackling a problem in geometry (and not just any way) make up a system of gymnastics of the attention calculated to give it greater aptitude for prayer.

Method for understanding images, symbols, etc. Not to try to interpret them, but to look at them till the light suddenly dawns.

Generally speaking, a method for the exercise of the intelligence, which consists of looking.

Application of this rule for the discrimination between the real and the illusory. In our sense perceptions, if we are not sure of what we see we change our position while looking, and what is real becomes evident. In the inner life, time takes the place of space. With time we are altered, and, if as we change we keep our gaze directed towards the same thing, in the end illusions are scattered and the real becomes visible. This is on condition that the attention be a looking and not an attachment.

When a struggle goes on between the will attached to some obligation and a bad desire, there is wearing away of the energy attached to good. We have to endure the biting of the desire passively, as we do a suffering which brings home to us our wretchedness, and we have to keep our attention turned towards the good. Then the quality of our energy is raised to a higher degree.

We must steal away the energy from our desires by taking away from them their temporal orientation.

Our desires are infinite in their pretensions but limited by the energy from which they proceed. That is why with the help of grace we can become their master and finally destroy them by attrition. As soon as this has been clearly understood, we have virtually conquered them, if we keep our attention in contact with this truth.

Video meliora . . . In such states, it seems as though we were thinking of the good, and in a sense we are doing so, but we are not thinking of its possibility.

It is incontestable that the void which we grasp with the pincers of contradiction is from on high, for we grasp it the better the more we sharpen our natural faculties of intelligence, will and love. The void which is from below is that into which we fall when we allow our natural faculties to become atrophied.

Experience of the transcendent: this seems contradictory, and yet the transcendent can be known only through contact since our faculties are unable to prevent it.

Solitude. Where does its value lie? For in solitude we are in the presence of mere matter (even the sky, the stars, the moon, trees in blossom), things of less value (perhaps) than a human spirit. Its value lies in the greater possibility of attention. If we could be attentive to the same degree in the presence of a human being . . .

We can only know one thing about God—that he is what we are not. Our wretchedness alone is an image of this. The more we contemplate it, the more we contemplate him.

Sin is nothing else but the failure to recognize human wretchedness. It is unconscious wretchedness and for that very reason guilty wretchedness. The story of Christ is the experimental proof that human wretchedness is irreducible, that it is as great in the absolutely sinless man as in the sinner. But in him who is without sin it is enlightened . . .

The recognition of human wretchedness is difficult for whoever is rich and powerful because he is almost invincibly led to believe that he is something. It is equally difficult for the man in miserable circumstances because he is almost invincibly led to believe that the rich and powerful man is something.

It is not the fault which constitutes mortal sin, but the degree of light in the soul when the fault, whatever it may be, is accomplished.

Purity is the power to contemplate defilement.

Extreme purity can contemplate both the pure and the impure: impurity can do neither: the pure frightens it, the impure absorbs it. It has to have a mixture.

Flannery O'Connor
(1925–1964)

Southern eccentric and Catholic writer, caretaker of
peacocks, suffering from lupus, Flannery O'Connor
was an extraordinary person. O'Connor's fictions are
dense parables, and the starkness of the evil and the
obscurity of the good in them have made them off-
putting for readers who have approached her work
expecting something more, well, obvious. O'Connor
lived on a farm, Andalusia, in Milledgeville, Georgia,
with her mother and her many peacocks and peahens.
The southern landscape is the backdrop of many of
her stories, and her characters often speak with a
drawl one can more easily identify if one has lived
below the Mason-Dixon line. Her work pits good
against evil as clearly as Milton's *Paradise Lost* pits
Satan against humanity, and as in Milton's epic poem,
O'Connor's evil is sometimes seductive, sometimes
mistaken by the characters it encounters, and perhaps by the reader as well. Like Milton's Satan,
O'Connor's manifestations of evil also have moments
of clarity and might also prompt other characters
towards revelation and salvation.

The letters below, to her friend, "A," show
O'Connor's concerns and ideas for her work, as well as
her own thoughts on theology. She was a philosopher
more than a mystic, and strongly disciplined in her
faith.

To "A."

2 August 1955

Thank you for writing me again. I feel I should apologize for
answering so promptly because I may seem to force on you a
correspondence that you don't have time for or that will
become a burden. I myself am afflicted with time, as I do not
work out on account of an energy-depriving ailment and my
work in, being creative, can go on only a few hours a day. I live
on a farm and don't see many people. My avocation is raising
peacocks, something that requires everything of the peacock
and nothing of me, so time is always at hand.

I try to believe too that there is only one Reality and that
that is the end of it, but the term, "Christian Realism," has
become necessary for me, perhaps in a purely academic way,
because I find myself in a world where everybody has his
compartment, puts you in yours, shuts the door and departs.
One of the awful things about writing when you are a Christian
is that for you the ultimate reality is the Incarnation, the present reality is the Incarnation, and nobody believes in the
Incarnation; that is, nobody in your audience. My audience
are the people who think God is dead. At least these are the
people I am conscious of writing for.

As for Jesus' being a realist: if He was not God, He was no
realist, only a liar, and the crucifixion an act of justice.

Dogma can in no way limit a limitless God. The person
outside the Church attaches a different meaning to it than the
person in. For me a dogma is only a gateway to contemplation
and is an instrument of freedom and not of restriction. It preserves mystery for the human mind. Henry James said the
young woman of the future would know nothing of mystery or
manners. He had no business to limit it to one sex.

You are right that I won't ever be able entirely to understand my own work or even my own motivations. It is first of

all a gift, but the direction it has taken has been because of the Church in me or the effect of the Church's teaching, not because of a personal perception or love of God. For you to think this would be possible is because of your ignorance of me; for me to think it would be sinful in a high degree. I am not a mystic and I do not lead a holy life. Not that I can claim any interesting or pleasurable things (my sense of the devil is strong) but I know all about the garden variety, pride, gluttony, envy, sloth, and what is more to the point, my virtues are as timid as my vices. I think sin occasionally brings one closer to God, but not habitual sin and not this petty kind that blocks every small good. A working knowledge of the devil can be very well had from resisting him.

However, the individual in the Church is, no matter how worthless himself, a part of the Body of Christ and a participator in the Redemption. There is no blueprint that the Church gives for understanding this. It is a matter of faith and the Church can force no one to believe it. When I ask myself how I know I believe, I have no satisfactory answer at all, no assurance at all, no feeling at all. I can only say with Peter, Lord I believe, help my unbelief. All I can say about my love of God is, Lord help me in my lack of it. I distrust pious phrases, particularly when they issue from my mouth. I try militantly never to be affected by the pious language of the faithful but it is always coming out when you least expect it. In contrast to the pious language of the faithful, the liturgy is beautifully flat.

I am wondering if you have read Simone Weil. I never have and doubt if I would understand her if I did; but from what I have read about her, I think she must have been a very great person. She and Edith Stein are the two 20th-century women who interest me most.

Whether you are a Christian or not, we both worship the God Who Is. St. Thomas on his death bed said of the *Summa*, "It's all straw,"—this was in the vision of that God.

6 September 1955

I looked in my Webster's and see it is 1948, so you are five years ahead of me in your vocabulary and I'll have to concede you the word. But I can't concede that I'm a fascist. The thought is probably more repugnant to me than to you, as I see it as an offense against the body of Christ. I am wondering why you convict me of believing in the use of force? It must be because you connect the Church with a belief in the use of force; but the Church is a mystical body which cannot, does not, believe in the use of force (in the sense of forcing conscience, denying the rights of conscience, etc.). I know all her hair-raising history, of course, but principle must be separated from policy. Policy and politics generally go contrary to principle. I in principle do not believe in the use of force, but I might well find myself using it, in which case I would have to convict myself of sin. I believe and the Church teaches that God is as present in the idiot boy as in the genius.

Of course I do not connect the Church exclusively with the Patriarchal Ideal. The death of such would not be the death of the Church, which is only now a seed and a Divine one. The things that you think she will be added to, will be added to her. In the end we visualize the same thing but I see it happening through Christ and His Church.

But I can never agree with you that the Incarnation, or any truth, has to satisfy emotionally to be right (and I would not agree that for the natural man the Incarnation does not satisfy emotionally). It does not satisfy emotionally for the person brought up under many forms of false intellectual disciplines such as 19th-century mechanism, for instance. Leaving the Incarnation aside, the very notion of God's existence is not emotionally satisfactory anymore for great numbers of people, which does not mean that God ceases to exist. M. Sartre finds God emotionally unsatisfactory in the extreme, as do most of my friends of less stature than he. The truth does not change according to our ability to stomach it emotionally. A higher paradox confounds emotion as well as reason and there are long periods in the lives of all of us, and of the saints, when the truth as revealed by faith is hideous, emotionally disturbing, and downright repulsive. Witness the dark night of the soul in individual saints. Right now the whole world seems to be going through a dark night of the soul.

There is a question whether faith can or is supposed to be emotionally satisfying. I must say that the thought of everyone lolling about in an emotionally satisfying faith is repugnant to me. I believe that we are ultimately directed Godward but that this journey is often impeded by emotion. I don't think you are a jellyfish. But I suspect you of being a Romantic. Which is not such an opprobrious thing as being a fascist. I do hope you will reconsider and relieve me of the burden of being a fascist. The only force I believe in is prayer, and it is a force I apply with more doggedness than attention.

To see Christ as God and man is probably no more difficult today than it has always been, even if today there seem to be more reasons to doubt. For you it may be a matter of not being able to accept what you call a suspension of the laws of the flesh and the physical, but for my part I think that when I know what the law of the flesh and the physical really are, then I will know what God is. We know them as we see them, but not as God sees them. For me, it is the virgin birth, the Incarnation, the resurrection which are the true laws of the flesh and the physical. Death, decay, destruction are the suspension of these laws. I am always astonished at the emphasis the Church puts on the body. It is not only the soul she says that will rise but the body, glorified. I have always thought that purity was the most mysterious of virtues, but it occurs to me that it would never have entered the human consciousness to conceive of purity if we were not to look forward to a resurrection of the body, which will be flesh and spirit united in peace, in the way they were in Christ. The resurrection of Christ seems the high point of nature . . .

Nancy Mairs
(1943–)

In her spiritual autobiography, *Ordinary Time*, in which the selection below appears, Nancy Mairs explores what it means to be a feminist and a Catholic. She also grapples with a number of other things: her own increasingly crippled body as she suffers from multiple sclerosis, her husband being diagnosed with a metastatic tumor, both of their previous infidelities, parenthood, and more. Mairs received a Ph.D. in English from the University of Arizona in 1984. She writes poetry and nonfiction, teaches writing, and lectures around the country. In the selection below, she usefully revises a popular notion of charity as those with more giving to those "less fortunate," explaining that everyone has abundances and that those receiving are giving something as well.

Charity is a tricky concept. At its root, which is shared with "cherish," the word suggests no ordinary indiscriminate affection but the love of something precious (costly, dear). Why then has it come to imply condescension? As with so many other ideas pertaining to relationships, our vast cultural passion for hierarchy must be at work. And where did that come from, I often wonder: out of the forest primeval, where if I perched in a tree while you skulked on the ground, I could more readily make you my lunch than you could make me yours? But that was quite a while ago. My mouth no longer waters when I glimpse you, even at lunchtime. Isn't it time we

dismantled a structure that so poorly organizes human inter-
actions? Not that this would be an easy task. Our language,
and the consciousness it shapes, is permeated with figures of
domination and subordination so thoroughly that if we tried to
extricate them, the whole fabric might unravel and leave us
gibbering, unable to construct a single coherent thought.

It's a risk we'll have to take, I think, if we are to survive as
recognizably human(e) beings in a world of finite resources.
Of course, nothing guarantees that we *are* to survive, and a
good bit of recent evidence suggests we aren't, but I think we
ought to give survival a shot. I'm not talking about "hanging in
there." I'm not talking about a few minor adjustments, or even
a lot of major adjustments. I'm not talking about a new world
order that permits Iraqi women and children to be bombed at
the command of rich white men just as Vietnamese women
and children were under the old world order, only more effi-
ciently and with wider approval. I am talking about an
upheaval so radical that it exalts every valley and makes the
rough places a plain, not along the San Andreas Fault but in
the human psyche, which will no longer choose (not desire—it
may well still desire—but choose) to organize itself and its
relationships with others in terms of power and rank.

We might begin where all things begin, with God. We need
to revise the language that we use to conceptualize God in
relation to ourselves. No more "Lord" and "Master." No more
"thrones" or "principalities." No more oracular pronounce-
ments "from on high." God with (in, among, beside, around,
not over and above) us. This is one of the reasons that I've
trained myself (and I balked badly at first) to refer to God with
the feminine pronoun. I don't think God is a woman, any
more than I think she's a man, but we're stuck with gendered
language: God has got to be a he, she, or it. As a woman, I now
feel most comfortable with "she" because traditionally in my
culture women have not occupied positions of political domi-
nance, associations with which might corrupt my experience
of the holy, and because I identify with her, thus becoming

aware of her presence in me, more readily when I use the same pronoun generally used for me. For a long time I considered changing "God," trying out "Goddess," "Holy One," "Yahweh," and the like, but they always felt contrived. Sometimes repeating "God" instead of using any pronoun is effective, but frequent repetitions at short intervals, by calling attention to themselves, distract me. The shift to the feminine pronoun seems to do the trick.

The purpose in finding a comfortable mode of address is to become aware of God drawn "down" into the midst of us, by whatever means will work. If she abides there, then the love we feel both for her and for one another as we embody her moves laterally, not hierarchically, and charity can never be tainted by condescension. When I use the word, I never intend it to suggest the act of "do-gooder" who gives a "hand-out" or a "hand-me-down" to someone "less fortunate" than himself; no matter what decency and good will both donor and recipient may feel, that "less" in the consciousness of one or both ineluctably skews their relationship. Charity is not a matter of degree. It is never nice. It wells up out of a sense of abundance, spilling indiscriminately outward. True, your abundance may complement someone else's lack, which you are moved to fill, but since your lacks are being similarly filled, perhaps by the same person, perhaps by another, reciprocity rather than domination frames the interchanges. Some people may be "more" fortunate and some "less," by whatever standard you choose. But absolutely everyone has abundances.

Of course, an abundance may not take the form you much like. I recall stopping, one blazing afternoon several years ago, at the Time Market for a carton of milk. Outside I was approached by a man wearing a few clothes and fewer teeth and a lot of sweat (life on the street in Tucson in midsummer is grueling), who asked me for a dollar. In those days, I didn't give money to people on the street because I knew they'd spend it on booze and I felt guilty assisting their addiction. Later, I was persuaded by the example of my beloved mentor

Jerry Robinett that my task was to give what I was asked for, leaving responsibility for the use of my gift to its recipient. But on this day I still thought of myself as a moral guardian, so I shook my head. Inside, as was my habit when I'd been pan-handled, I bought in addition to my milk a large apple and a granola bar (oh, the smugness of us virtuous types—why the hell not a red Popsicle and a Twinkie?).

When I offered these to the man outside, he snarled and turned his back. He'd been joined by a friend, who said to him quietly, "You know her. From the Casa. Go on and take them." He just shook his head, so I extended them to the friend, who took them and smiled. There was genuine grace in his gesture, his reluctance to hurt the feelings of a woman he's seen at the soup kitchen, and I welcomed that gift from his abundance. But the other had an abundance, too—an abundance of resentment—from which he'd given just as freely. I was chas-tened by the gift, by his refusal to say, "Thank you, kind lady," accepting my stupid health food when all he really wanted was a cold six pack. If he'd done that, I'd never have found out that I'd offered him the wrong thing. I might have gone on believ-ing that poor people were obliged to take what I gave them, consider themselves lucky to get it, and probably thank me politely in the bargain. I never said you had to *like* getting your lacks filled. I just said that someone, out of his abundance, would take care of the job.

Under ordinary circumstances, our abundances need let-ting off, like steam, and the family model chosen by contem-porary middle-class society, wherein the whole huge human family is fragmented into clusters of only a few members each, which are packed separately and antiseptically, like cans of peas or jars of pickles, into houses and apartments and mini-vans, lacks adequate amplitude and ventilation. Accumulated, hoarded, our abundances build up an excruciating pressure that we seek to relieve in material acquisition, but the relief this measure brings is always only temporary, and eventually we find ourselves stopped up and sick with things.

I'm not preaching from a lofty perch here, looking down in pity on the rest of you poor fools gagging on your glut. I'm gasping claustrophobically under the weight on my own heap of possessions. Look! Down here! Under the three pairs of boots and the second television set! Admittedly, the boots are different colors to complement different articles in my wardrobe, and the television is a black-and-white portable with a five-inch screen: I'm a practical accumulator. But maybe color-coordination is not a laudable end or even a reasonable goal, and no one except my sports-crazy stepfather attempts to watch more than one television at a time. What am I really doing with all this stuff?

I know what I should do with it. I accept Jesus's admonition to the rich young man: "If you would be perfect, go, sell what you possess and give to the poor, and you will have treasure in heaven; come, follow me" (Matt. 19.21). I know that such actions can be carried out, because I have friends who have done so. And I like to think I have developed to the point that, if only I were healthy and vigorous, I could do the same. If only . . . Here's where I get stuck. I am too debilitated now to hold a job or even to care fully for myself. My husband has metastatic melanoma. When he dies, the modest resources we've accumulated may not even provide for my shelter and custodial care. If I were to give them away, then I'd become a public burden, worse than useless even to the poor I sought to serve. Conserving them seems less like greed than like social responsibility. And so I get off lightly. I can indulge in the fantasy that, under different circumstances, I would be "perfect" without ever having to put myself to the test, a saint manquée.

Well, what I would do if I could we'll never know. I must do what I can. Carrying out the injunction that closes every Mass, to "go in peace to love and serve God and our neighbor," takes the form of the works of mercy, seven of which are "corporal": (1) to feed the hungry, (2) to give drink to the thirsty, (3) to clothe the naked, (4) to visit the imprisoned, (5) to shelter the homeless, (6) to visit the sick, and (7) to bury the dead. Another seven are "spiritual": (1) to admonish the sinner, (2) to instruct the ignorant, (3) to counsel the doubtful, (4) to comfort the sorrowful, (5) to bear wrongs patiently, (6) to forgive all injuries, and (7) to pray for the living and the dead. "As far as I can tell, I'm supposed to do all of these," I say to [my husband] George, "but some of the spiritual ones make me uneasy. They seem so presumptuous." He nods as I go on: "I'd rather just clothe the sinner"—we burst out laughing and say together—"and admonish the naked."

Seriously, at the risk of spiritual dereliction, I think I'll leave admonishment to someone with more of a flair for it and stick with bodies, their shelter and nurture and dispatch, for which a quarter of a century of mothering all creatures great and small has better fitted me. Let me feed the hungry. Let me clothe the naked (and sinners too). I won't do it well or often enough, I know from experience, but charity isn't a competition to be judged by the Big Examiner in the Sky, who'll knock off seven years of purgatory for every sack of groceries you drop off at the Community Food Bank. Nobody's looking. It's more like a game in which everyone gets a turn, or a dance for which everyone can choreograph a few steps. Even a woman too crippled to tie her own boots or drive a car can, at least if she has a partner who shares her sense of plenty, find a place in the vast web of transactions that binds and sustains the human family.

In such exchanges, no matter how equitable, the power of the giver to dispense or withhold some good is subtly privileged over the right of the receiver to accept or reject the offering by the fact of possession: you've got what I need. Even though I've long understood this distinction, only in recent years have I felt its force. What I need—repetitively, interminably—is help in performing even the most elementary tasks. I can't butter my own bread. Before long I may not even be able to use the toilet by myself. My dependency, in resembling that of a very young child, makes me feel demeaned, diminished, humiliated. This is a horrible situation, one that wracks me with grief and fury for which no socially acceptable outlet exists. What am I going to do if you offer to button my coat, after all—bite your fingers and then freeze to death? Of course not. I'm going to permit you to clothe the naked.

Horrible situations have their uses, however. Mine, in depriving me of the status associated with personal control, has forced humility upon me. I cannot patronize the poor. Currently, my poverty isn't economic, though it may one day be that as well, but its effects are similar. I must be not only the agent but the object of the works of mercy. I must discipline myself to accept and welcome others' care. I wish I could tell you that I'm doing a terrific job of it, that I'm just the sweetest, humblest little woman you've ever met, but I can't. All I can say is that, in learning to give care whenever I can and receive care whenever I must, I've grown more attentive to the personal dimension of the works of mercy.

Anne Lamott
(1954–)

Anne Lamott is known for her frank, funny, insightful
writing. She grew up in California's Bay area where she
raised her son and continues to reside. She has overcome and written about her experiences with alcohol-
ism and depression, and her conversion, described in
the first selection below, was one of the important life
changes that enabled her to overcome these obstacles.
She became a single parent, and her relationship with
her son, Sam, is the subject of much of her work, as in
the second selection below.

[*A depressive alcoholic, Lamott had just had an abortion. She
describes a step in her conversion process during her
recovery.*]

Several hours later, the blood stopped flowing, and I got in
bed, shaky and sad and too wild to have another drink or take
another sleeping pill. I had a cigarette and turned off the light.
After a while, as I lay there, I became aware of someone with
me, hunkered down in the corner, and I just assumed it was
my father, whose presence I had felt over the years when I was
frightened and alone. The feeling was so strong that I actually
turned on the light for a moment to make sure no one was
there—of course, there wasn't. But after a while, in the dark
again, I knew beyond any doubt that it was Jesus. I felt him as
surely as I feel my dog lying nearby as I write this.

And I was appalled. I thought about my life and my brilliant hilarious progressive friends, I thought about what
everyone would think of me if I became a Christian, and it
seemed an utterly impossible thing that simply could not be
allowed to happen. I turned to the wall and said out loud, "I
would rather die."

I felt him just sitting there on his haunches in the corner of
my sleeping loft, watching me with patience and love, and I
squinched my eyes shut, but that didn't help because that's not
what I was seeing him with.

Finally I fell asleep, and in the morning, he was gone.

This experience spooked me badly, but I thought it was
just an apparition, born of fear and self-loathing and booze
and loss of blood. But then everywhere I went, I had the feeling that a little cat was following me, wanting me to reach
down and pick it up, wanting me to open the door and let it
in. But I knew what would happen: you let a cat in one time,
give it a little milk, and then it stays forever. So I tried to keep
one step ahead of it, slamming my houseboat door when I
entered or left.

And one week later, when I went back to church, I was so
hungover that I couldn't stand up for the songs, and this time
I stayed for the sermon, which I thought was so ridiculous,
like someone trying to convince me of the existence of extra-
terrestrials, but the last song was so deep and raw and pure
that I could not escape. It was as if the people were singing in
between the notes, weeping and joyful at the same time, and
I felt like their voices or *something* was rocking me in its
bosom, holding me like a scared kid, and I opened up to that
feeling—and it washed over me.

I began to cry and left before the benediction, and I raced
home and felt the little cat running along at my heels, and I
walked down the dock past dozens of potted flowers, under a
sky as blue as one of God's own dreams, and I opened the door
to my houseboat, and I stood there a minute, and then I hung

my head and said, "Fuck it: I quit." I took a long deep breath and said out loud, "All right. You can come in."

So this was my beautiful moment of conversion.

> And here in the dust and dirt, O here,
> The lilies of his love appear.

I started to find these lines of George Herbert's everywhere I turned—in Simone Weil, Malcolm Muggeridge, books of English poetry. Meanwhile, I trooped back and forth through the dust and grime of the flea market every Sunday morning till eleven, when I crossed the street from the market to the church.

I was sitting through the sermon now every week and finding that I could not only bear the Jesus talk but was interested, searching for clues. I was more and more comfortable with the radical message of peace and equality, with the God in whom Dr. King believed. I had no big theological thoughts, but had discovered that if I said, Hello?, to God, I could *feel* God say, Hello, back. It was like being in a relationship with Casper. Sometimes I wadded up a Kleenex and held it tightly in one fist so that it felt like I was walking hand in hand with him.

[*This is an excerpt from a longer essay; here, Lamott is ticketed for walking her dog without a leash and she goes home to wake her teenage son so he can join her for a church service she helps to administer weekly at a local convalescent home.*]

"What if I were to tell you that she's not actually my dog?" I asked. The men smiled. I looked at Lily. "I've never seen that dog in my life."

Lily bounded over to me with her branch and flung herself against my leg, staring up at me, a furry, panting Saint John the Divine.

On the lower part of the path home, new grass wasn't growing yet. The short golden grass lay flattened by weather, in swirls of hat hair.

It was after one when I got home. There was progress: Sam was now asleep on the upstairs couch.

I roused him. "We have to leave in an hour," I said. "And I told you to get your chores done before we go."

"Give me ten more minutes!" he cried. And remembering how the cops had made me feel, I let him sleep.

My friend Neshama arrived. She was going with us. I pantomimed choking my sleeping child. Then I made sandwiches for us all. She and I ate.

At ten of two, I shook Sam again. "Get up now," I said. I was about to shout at him. But he looked like a skinny marine mammal, washed ashore.

Another of the four things I know for sure about raising kids is that most times when you overlook bad behavior, or let them blow you off when something is important to you, you injure them. You hobble their character.

The third of the four things I know is that if you can shine a small beam of truth on a beloved when you are angry, it is more beneficial than hitting that beloved with a klieg light of feelings and pinning the person to the wall. I can't remember the fourth, but I put numbers 2 and 3 into practice.

I closed my eyes, gathered myself, bent down and spoke to my son calmly.

"Sam? You've said several times you would come with me today. I want you to, but I don't want to make myself crazy trying to get you to live up to your promises. If it doesn't happen, I'm going to be sad and angry, but I am not going to lose myself in your bullshit."

He got up and went downstairs to his room, grumpily. Neshama looked at me.

"You did great," she said. I closed my eyes and let my head drop to my chest. We heard Sam's footsteps on the stairs coming toward us.

The three of us went outside and got in the car, Sam in the backseat, where he ate his sandwich in sleepy silence.

There were only six residents waiting in the recreation room for us to begin the service, five women and one man, fragile as onion skin. There were five of us from church, plus Neshama, so I assigned everyone a resident to shepherd through the short service. We always sing a few songs, say a few prayers, take the residents' hands and look in their eyes and say, "The peace of God be with you." Sam accompanied a pretty Asian woman, who talked to him as if he might be one of her relatives. He introduced himself to her shyly. "Yes," she said happily. "Sam." He took his place at her side. For the next half-hour, he turned the pages of the worship book for her and ran his fingers along the words of each hymn so she could follow. He's been coming here with me off and on his whole life, because I so believe in this ministry and want him to share it with me: the people here are shipwrecks, and sometimes there is not much left, but there is a thread in them that can be pulled and that still vibrates. It's like being with nuns who have taken vows of silence and mutter. So we show up, talk, and sing. It seems to fill the residents, breathe more life into them. Sam's companion beamed and concentrated on doing her parts correctly, as if to please him. When we sang "Jesus Loves Me," a song she and the others may have learned as children, some sang along, muttering and murmuring like brooks: there's such pleasure in knowing the words to a song.

I've seen them come back to life during this service, even when they cannot sing. I've seen these moments bring them joy and comfort. We don't lay a heavy Jesus trip on anyone: it's more that he is a medium for our showing up and caring.

My person was sound asleep. I was beginning to think it was the effect I have on people. She was wearing a bright red sweatsuit and could not have weighed more than eighty pounds. When she finally woke up, I greeted her.

"I want to go back to sleep," she cried out, and I assured her that that was okay. I took her hands and she babbled for a minute. "I like that house," she said, and I held on to her hands. Sam came over. "She wants to sleep," he whispered, "because she liked the house in her dreams."

"That's exactly right," I said. He went back to the Asian woman. My woman in red fell asleep again. I continued with a prayer.

Some of the residents seemed to be out of it, drooling, dazed. Then you would hear them saying the Lord's Prayer, "*Amen,*" we say loudly; then we go around one last time, touch each person, and tell them how glad we are that they are there. I realize again and again that this is really all you have to offer people most days, a touch, a moment's gladness. It has to do, and it often does.

"Hey, thanks," I told Sam as we headed outside with Neshama.

"No problem," he said. We walked to my car. "I liked my person," he added. His hair was matted down in bed-head tufts, like the hills.

Heidi Neumark
(1954–)

The Lutheran pastor at the Transfiguration Church in the South Bronx until 2003, Heidi Neumark's indelible description of the church and community in which she found herself in the eighties is remarkable. Her narrative, *Breathing Space*, from which the selection below was taken, depicts people living in a time and place that might inspire despair in the strongest of souls; yet, Neumark and her congregation maintain and grow their faith and hope together, despite the odds against them. Neumark graduated from Brown and received her degree in Divinity from the Lutheran Theological Seminary in Philadelphia. Her writing is smart, graceful, and insightful, as the selection below demonstrates.

The demographics of this neighborhood favor the young, but there are still elderly members to visit. While I needed to immerse myself in the neighborhood, it didn't mean forgetting about the folks who'd held the church together for so many years. When I arrived, Alma was one of the few members who still lived in the area. In her nineties, she loved to walk. She invented daily errands to get out on the streets. She often went to visit friends unlikely to be home. Whenever we announced the need for chaperones on a youth outing, Alma raised her hand. Then she was confined to bed with a missing leg, amputated because of her diabetes. When she came out of surgery, I found her in the hallway, still groggy from anesthesia. As soon as she saw me, she smiled: "How are your children, Pastor?" "How is your husband?" This is typical. I know of many pastors who feel that ministry is a one-way street; they give, but they don't get, at least not from their parishioners. My experience here is utterly different. I am given far more than I can give, and those doing the giving are often perceived by most as the neediest of all, folks looking for hand-outs. On balance, I find many more hands here are stretched out to give than to take.

I went to visit Alma again when she came home from the hospital. Before we prayed, it was important for her to lift the bed covers, unwrap the long strips of gauze and bare the stump where her leg used to be, so that in praying, I might see her wound, her loss. At the end of the visit, she touched the metal railing of the bed, smiled widely, and said, "this is my cradle now."

The next time I saw Alma, she didn't know where she was. In her mind, she was still in the old Bronx neighborhood, but in fact she had been moved to a nursing home in Brooklyn. She sat in her wheelchair, parked in the hallway, and I found a loose chair for myself. Soon we mercifully left the confusing corridor with its urine-soaked diapers and entered the limpid geography of the Psalter. Once there, Alma knew every turn and detail of the landscape. The hills rose with familiar grace. She moved unimpeded across this holy land and her mind leapt up in its glorious lucidity.

Most of the 150 Psalms seem etched into her DNA—not just memorized but woven through the very strands of Alma's being. *Alzaré mis ojos a los montes. ¿De dónde vendrá mi socorro? Mi socorro viene de Jehová que hizo los cielos y la tierra. (I lift up my eyes to the hills—from where will my help come? My help comes from the Lord who made heaven and earth.* Psalm 121:1–2) Together we roamed the hills, free of wheelchairs, prostheses and canes, leaning on the everlasting arms.

●●●

I visited Mirta who was hospitalized after an asthma attack. It was hard for her to be in the same hospital where her mother, Cordelia, had recently died of AIDS, after years of drug abuse. Near the end, Cordelia wondered if it was too late to receive her First Communion. Of course not. "But I haven't done the class," she worried. No matter. What matters is the hunger. She wanted to confess and receive absolution, the Communion. *This is the body of Christ, given for you. This is the blood of Christ, shed for you.* Cordelia lay in the white sheets, smiling. *"Gracias,"* she said, *"gracias."* It was the last word I heard her speak.

I think Mirta's grieving contributed to her hospital admission. I sat with her as she lay in bed, wheezing and struggling for air, and reflected on the powerful kinship between this illness that constricts the passage of breath and the struggle for silence and prayer in my own life. So often, I wheeze and am brought low by stress, all the environmental irritants that swirl invisibly through my life evading awareness. Like Mirta, I've found myself weakened and debilitated, again and again. Perhaps I simply need to accept this and get on. "Prayer is a battle all the way to the last breath," said one of the Desert Fathers, Abba Agathon.

Physical breath, metaphysical breath—I think they belong together. In the Genesis creation story, God breathes over the waters, and chaos swirls into shape. God breathes the *ruah*, or holy wind of life, into human beings, which propels them to their feet. In Hebrew, *ruah* is feminine, what the poet Gerard Manley Hopkins called "world-mothering air." What this story communicates to me is that life is holy, all of it.

Ezekiel saw the same thing when he pictured his community as a field of dry bones:

> Suddenly there was a noise, a rattling, and the bones
> came together, bone to its bone. I looked, and there

were sinews on them, and flesh had come upon them,
and skin had covered them; but there was no breath in
them. (Ezekiel 37:7–8a)

At first, the bones link up in their individual skeletal frame-
works. But as bodies disconnected from one another, without
community, they still can't move. They're all fitted out with
sinews and skin, going nowhere. *"Come from the four winds,
O breath,"* cries the prophet, *"and the breath came into them,
and they lived, and stood on their feet, a vast multitude."* Like
Ezekiel's bones, we might rattle through the motions, but
without *ruah*-spirit-breath, nothing gets up or moves forward.
Space becomes claustrophobic, literally a closed-in place
where fear sucks out the air. Many people shut in their project
apartments feel like this—isolated with no exit. The welfare
system does it, too, knocks the wind out.

It's the same place Jesus' disciples found themselves in after
his death, like the locked church where I first met
Transfiguration's members huddled together:

> The doors of the house where the disciples had met
> were locked for fear . . . Jesus came and stood among
> them and said . . . "Peace be with you. As the Father
> has sent me, so I send you." When he had said this, he
> breathed on them. (John 20:19, 21–22)

It was breath that set them free to open breathing space for
others.

* * *

Mirta can do little to change the conditions in the small apart-
ment she shares with her grandmother, aunt, and two brothers. The doctor wrote a letter urging the aunt to limit her
smoking to outside the building. When I asked Mirta about it,
she threw up her hands. Her aunt tried for a few days, but
smoking in the hallway was not like sitting on the couch with

a cup of coffee. Soon she went right back to chain-smoking in the living room. I, on the other hand, have options. I can do things that I don't do. I am, as Auden puts it, "craving the sensation but ignoring the cause."

The doctors prescribed a new pump for Mirta. They thought it would work better than the bulky machine she'd been dragging around in case of an attack. What should I take for emergencies with this asthma of the spirit? I hope Pope Pius V doesn't mind recurring use of his prayer by a Lutheran: "Have mercy on your people, Lord, and give us a breathing space in the midst of so many troubles."

Acknowledgements

Excerpts from *Handbook for William, A Carolingian Woman's Counsel for Her Son* by Dhuoda, translated by Carol Neel, reprinted by permission of the University of Nebraska Press. Copyright © 1991 by the University of Nebraska Press.

Excerpts from *Scivias* by Hildegard of Bingen, translated by Mother Columba Hart and Jane Bishop, Paulist Press, Inc., New York/Mahwah, NJ. Reprinted by permission of Paulist Press, Inc. www.paulistpress.com

Excerpts from *Elisabeth of Schönau, The Complete Works*; translated and introduced by Anne L. Clark, copyright © 2000 by Anne L. Clark, Paulist Press, Inc., New York/Mahwah, NJ. Reprinted by permission of Paulist Press, Inc. www.paulist-press.com

The Revelations of St. Birgitta of Sweden, Vo. II, translated by Denis Searby (2006). Selection reprinted by permission of Oxford University Press, USA.

The Book of the City of Ladies, by Christine de Pizan. Translated by Earl Jeffrey Richards. Copyright © 1982 by Persea Books, Inc. Selection reprinted by permission of Persea Books, Inc., New York. All rights reserved.

The Shewings of Julian of Norwich, edited by Georgia Ronan Crampton, Middle English Texts Series (Kalamazoo, MI: